Get Started on your Mac

T0186946

Get Started on your Mac

Rod Lawton

For UK order enquiries: please contact Bookpoint Ltd, 130 Milton Park, Abingdon, Oxon OX14 4SB. Telephone: +44 (0) 1235 827720. Fax: +44 (0) 1235 400454. Lines are open 09.00–17.00, Monday to Saturday, with a 24-hour message answering service. Details about our titles and how to order are available at www.teachyourself.com

Long renowned as the authoritative source for self-guided learning – with more than 50 million copies sold worldwide – the Teach Yourself series includes over 500 titles in the fields of languages, crafts, hobbies, business, computing and education.

British Library Cataloguing in Publication Data: a catalogue record for this title is available from the British Library.

First published in UK 2010 by Hodder Education, part of Hachette UK, 338 Euston Road, London NW1 3BH.

The Teach Yourself name is a registered trade mark of Hodder Headline.

Copyright © Rod Lawton 2010

In UK: All rights reserved. Apart from any permitted use under UK copyright law, no part of this publication may be reproduced or transmitted in any form or by any means, electronic or mechanical, including photocopy, recording, or any information, storage and retrieval system, without permission in writing from the publisher or under licence from the Copyright Licensing Agency Limited. Further details of such licences (for reprographic reproduction) may be obtained from the Copyright Licensing Agency Limited, of Saffron House, 6–10 Kirby Street, London EC1N 8TS.

Typeset by MPS Limited, a Macmillan Company.

Printed in Great Britain for Hodder Education, an Hachette UK Company, 338 Euston Road, London NW1 3BH, by CPI Cox & Wyman, Reading, Berkshire RG1 8EX.

The publisher has used its best endeavours to ensure that the URLs for external websites referred to in this book are correct and active at the time of going to press. However, the publisher and the author have no responsibility for the websites and can make no guarantee that a site will remain live or that the content will remain relevant, decent or appropriate.

Hachette UK's policy is to use papers that are natural, renewable and recyclable products and made from wood grown in sustainable forests. The logging and manufacturing processes are expected to conform to the environmental regulations of the country of origin.

Impression number   10 9 8 7 6 5 4 3 2 1

Year   2014 2013 2012 2011 2010

Front cover: © Ingram Publishing Ltd

Back cover: © Jakub Semeniuk/iStockphoto.com, © Royalty-Free/ Corbis, © agencyby/iStockphoto.com, © Andy Cook/iStockphoto.com, © Christopher Ewing/iStockphoto.com, © zebicho – Fotolia.com, © Geoffrey Holman/iStockphoto.com, © Photodisc/Getty Images, © James C. Pruitt/iStockphoto.com, © Mohamed Saber – Fotolia.com

Contents

Welcome to *Get Started on your Mac*

This book is for anyone who's just bought a Mac or is thinking of buying one. It's written for people who are just getting started with computers, and more experienced users who've maybe got used to a PC and need to know what's different about a Mac. It starts off with the basics – how to choose a Mac, how they work and what they can do. And despite the visual differences, when it comes down to the basics, Macs and PCs are really very similar in what they do and how they do it.

PCs use the Windows operating system, while Macs use Mac OS X. Like Windows, this has gone through several versions, and the latest of these is OS X 10.6 'Snow Leopard'. It can be difficult in a book like this to cover new and older versions of the operating system at the same time, but the differences between this and OS X 10.5 'Leopard' aren't that great. Before that came OS X 10.4 'Tiger', and while this was a bigger jump, it's still not as great as Windows Vista to Windows 7, for example.

What this means is that while this book concentrates on the Snow Leopard operating system, there's often very little practical difference between this and Leopard, and much of what's written here, especially general advice about using computers and software applications, will apply to Tiger and even earlier versions of the Mac OS.

There are some technical sections in this book, but they've been kept to a minimum. The Mac is meant to be straightforward, intuitive and friendly, and that's the tone we've tried to adopt here. The aim is to show what you can do, how it works, and how to get started. Often the main barrier to learning something new is not in the technical detail, but in the broad understanding of what's going on and why.

There are specific chapters devoted to the software programs which come with the Mac, and they do deserve a close look because they are much more powerful and useful than most 'free' software. Macs might cost more than PCs to buy, but once you factor in the value of the software that comes with them, the cost equation changes. iPhoto, iCal, iTunes, iWeb and the rest are apparently simple programs with hidden depths. You really don't have to know very much to start using them, but they continue to keep up with you as your knowledge, expertise and requirements move on.

We also spend some time looking at Apple's office suite 'iWork'. It's a lot cheaper than Microsoft Office and looks a lot simpler too... but looks can be deceiving. Pages, Keynote and Numbers are very powerful office tools which can usually match and sometimes exceed the features in Microsoft Office.

We also look at the Mac version of Microsoft Office itself. This is an important suite for Mac owners who work in an office environment because it means they can swap files directly with PC users without worrying about file conversions or formatting problems. The bottom line is that the Mac can be just as effective as a business tool as it is a home computer.

You'll notice that there's nothing in this book about viruses and a limited amount on security in general. At the moment, viruses are not a problem for Mac users. Apple is inclined to be a little too smug about this at times, because it seems reasonable to assume that as soon as there are enough Macs on the market to make it a worthwhile target, the hackers won't be far behind. Debate rages in the technical community, too, about whether there are Mac viruses 'in the wild' or not. For now, though, it's something Mac owners don't have to deal with.

There are other security threats, such as 'phishing' emails that try to con you into revealing your bank account details and other personal information, but this is just common sense and not really a technical issue at all.

We've had to leave a few things out, including Apple's professional design applications and its role in the creative industries. That will have to wait for another book. We've also left out GarageBand, the excellent free music creation program that comes as part of the iLife suite. There was no room, either, for a more detailed look at Leopard's excellent iChat application and its revolutionary 'theatre' mode.

Instead, we've tried to concentrate on the most important things first. The main thing is not to get bogged down in the details. You want to know what you can do, whether it's easy and how to get started.

Only got a minute?

You've just walked into one of those swanky white-walled Apple stores. There are row upon row of Macs laid out for your inspection, and an eager associate waiting to give you a guided tour. Where do you start? What do you ask for? What do you need?

From the look of the shop it appears that there are about a million different Macs – but there aren't. Chapter 1, 'Choosing a Mac', breaks them all down into manageable chunks. In fact there are only four: the Mac Mini, the iMac, the MacBook and the Mac Pro. The reason there are so many laid out is that each type comes with variations in memory, processor, storage capacity and other features.

Choose the Mac Mini if you want a cheap introduction to Macs that works with your current monitor; the iMac as an elegant and powerful all-in-one Mac for the home or office; a Mac Pro if you're a design professional; or a MacBook if you want a laptop.

Once you've chosen which of these four most suits your needs, you've narrowed the choice down to something much more manageable, and your Apple Store associate can explain the rest. This is going to boil down to how much power you need and how much you want to spend. The main things you'll get thrown at you are processor speed, RAM and hard disk size.

The processor speed makes a difference, but any modern Mac is pretty fast already, so unless you're heavily into video or high-resolution photo editing, a basic model might be fine.

The more RAM, though, the better. Consider 2Gb a minimum and 3–4Gb as a better starting point. Most models let you add more if you need to, as well.

And the bigger the hard disk the better, too. Between 320–500Gb will get you started, but if you shoot and save a lot of videos, that will fill up pretty fast. Adding a bigger hard disk is trickier than adding more RAM, so it's worth considering a little extra outlay here.

In a nutshell, the big decision is choosing which of the four Mac models is right for you, and the rest is just details.

5 Only got five minutes?

You may be used to PCs, and the Mac can look very different to Windows, but these differences are superficial. Pretty well all the things you do on a PC have an equivalent on the Mac. There's more on this in Chapter 2, 'How Macs work', Chapter 4, 'Leopard and Snow Leopard', Chapter 8, 'Working with PCs', and elsewhere throughout this book.

When you start the Mac, it goes through the same start-up process as a PC, loading the operating system from the hard disk. It will then prompt you to choose a username and a password (if you've set one up) to log in with. It's the same on a PC, where you can set up different user accounts for different people.

Once it's started up, the Mac displays its desktop. It looks different to a PC's, but it's the same thing. You'll see icons for the hard disk and perhaps other items, depending on how the Mac's been set up.

PCs have a Start menu which you use to run applications. The Mac equivalent is the Dock. This is a toolbar fixed to the bottom or the side of the screen. The Dock contains icons for the various applications on the Mac, but you can customize it by removing those you don't want and adding others.

Where Windows has Windows Explorer for browsing through the contents of your computer, the Mac has the Finder. This works in a very similar way, displaying files and folders as icons or lists, depending on how you want to set it up. Double-clicking a folder icon will open the folder and double-clicking a file will open that file with the relevant extension.

PC files have extensions on the end to show the file type. Windows uses these to choose the correct application to open them with. The Mac embeds the file type information within the file, but often uses the extensions anyway so that files are compatible with PCs. This does mean that some Mac files will have extensions while others don't – it's only important, though, when swapping files with PCs.

Mac applications aren't compatible with PC applications. You have to buy the Mac version of any software application (if available) that you want to use. Most file types, however, are compatible. You can usually exchange digital image files (JPEGs, TIFFs and so on), movie files and even Microsoft Office files without problems, however. There is a version of Microsoft Office for the Mac, while Apple's own 'office' suite, iWork, can open and export Microsoft Office files too.

Macs are fully compatible with wired Ethernet networks and wireless routers. You don't need to get special versions of either. They can connect seamlessly with PCs over a network.

You don't have to rely on networks for file transfer. Although the hard disk format used by Macs is different to that used by PCs, they can both use the same FAT32 format for external hard disks and USB flash drives. You can copy files onto a flash drive on a Mac and then copy them on to a PC and vice versa.

At one time, Macs and PCs were incompatible, and trying to use both side-by-side could be time-consuming and difficult. Nowadays, it's completely different. There are still basic differences between them, but for the most part they can work alongside each other without difficulty. In no way are you cutting yourself off from the rest of the computing world by choosing a Mac, and if you use an iPod, iPad or iPhone, a Mac is the obvious choice. Even if you're used to a PC it won't take you long to realize the basic similarities between the two machines.

1

....

Choosing a Mac

In this chapter you will learn:
- *about the hardware specifications*
- *how much memory and hard disk space you need*
- *who the different Mac models are designed for*
- *which Mac is best for you*
- *about Mac versus PCs: the facts*

1.1 Processors

Choosing a computer is complicated if you have little interest in technicalities, and it's not much better even if you do know the difference between a processor and a peripheral, because the benchmarks are moving all the time. Besides, what's touted as a 'revolution' often turns out to be just a slight improvement on what went before. Don't forget that the primary purpose of any computer manufacturer is to sell more computers!

But you do need something to go on when weighing up one model versus another and deciding what to spend. And computers are generally judged on three components: the processor, the memory (RAM) and the hard disk size. These are the components that always head up the specs sheets in the store.

We'll start with the processor, which can be considered to be the computer's 'brain'. Processors are evolving all the time, and what's hot this year (dual core) will be next year's budget buy, so don't try to memorize the figures, just remember the principles.

Three things affect the processor performance: (a) the processor family (each generation is a leap forward from the last), (b) the operating system and hardware of the computer it's running on and (c) its clock speed, which is the rate at which it performs calculations.

You can visit the Apple Store via www.apple.com/uk to see the range of Mac configurations available. This makes it clearer how the range is broken down.

For example, if we go to the Apple website and check the specs of the cheapest Mac Mini we find that at the time of writing it has a Core 2 Duo processor (that's the chip family) running at 2.4GHz (gigahertz – that's the clock speed). By contrast, the top-of-the-range iMac has a Core 2 Duo running at 3.3GHz. We can expect the expensive iMac to work considerably faster than the cheap Mac Mini, then.

Mac Pros use a different processor family. Dual-core processors (two chips in one, essentially) aren't powerful enough for the high-end creative applications these computers are designed for, and they use a different quad-core chip family (Intel Xeon 3500 and 5500). The top model has two Intel Xeon quad-core chips (so it's an 8-core machine!) which run at a speed of 2.93GHz – slightly slower than the top iMac, then – but the quad-core design is intrinsically more powerful than the dual-core processor in the iMac.

Confused? Let's keep it simple, then. A better chip family usually gives you the biggest performance improvement, but if two computers use the same processor family, then you can judge which is the faster from the clock speed.

....

Author insight

There's no need to spend a fortune. Even a basic Mac Mini has far more power than a mid-range iMac a couple of years ago. The author's family is still happily using a Mac Mini 'solo' (single-core processor) that has just 1Gb RAM and is several years old. It gets used for email, web browsing, YouTube, FaceBook and school projects, and it's more than up to the job.

....

1.2 RAM

Processor speed, though, is not the sole factor in deciding performance. It doesn't matter how fast the computer's brain is if it has a tiny memory.

This is the RAM, or Random Access Memory. It's like the computer's thinking space. The more RAM it has the more things it can do at once.

All computers, Macs included, are sold with enough RAM to get you started, but they always work better with more. It is possible to buy and fit more RAM chips yourself, but it may be simpler to specify more memory when you order the machine – this prevents any quibbles over whether you've opened the machine up inside the warranty period.

Basic Mac Minis come with 2Gb RAM, which is actually adequate for most purposes, but there's space inside to increase this to 8Gb. This is actually good enough for many professional applications, an indication that the Mac Mini is now not just an entry-level computer.

iMacs now ship with 4Gb RAM. That's more generous than the Mac Mini's standard allocation, not because iMacs demand more RAM, but because their users are likely to be a little more ambitious in what they do and the programs they want to run. 4Gb is actually pretty generous, given that the vast majority of applications will run in 2Gb at a pinch. You can, however, increase the RAM up to 16Gb, and the top iMacs can be considered professional tools, not just home computers.

Apple doesn't specify a standard amount of RAM for the Mac Pros models. These are aimed at professionals, and it's expected that users will know how much RAM they want and will add it to their order. These machines can accommodate up to 32Gb of RAM.

So how much do you need? Well, for email, surfing, the iLife applications that come with the computer and general office jobs like word processing and so on, 2Gb is probably going to be fine. If you're interested in digital photography or digital video, you'll be better off with 4Gb of RAM. Professional applications in these areas are likely to work a little faster with 8Gb of RAM, especially if you are running more than one program at the same time. Beyond that you're into specialist territory that's outside the scope of this book.

Now the point about RAM is that if you don't have enough, you don't usually find that things refuse to work. That's because the Mac will get the extra memory it needs by temporarily using space on the hard disk – this is called 'virtual memory'. It's a neat idea that's also used by Windows on PCs. The problem is that by comparison with real (RAM) memory, it's terribly slow. Imagine you have a very poor memory yourself (maybe you don't need to imagine!) and you have to keep stopping what you're doing to write it down so that you can clear your mind for something else. That's what the computer's doing with virtual memory. It will work much faster if it doesn't have to keep stopping to write data to the disk and then read it back into the memory again later on.

Indeed, the amount of RAM can be just as big a factor in the computer's performance as the processor it uses. If you don't have enough RAM, your super-fast processor is going to spend much of its time kicking its heels and waiting for data.

Author insight

If you're into digital photography, digital video or any other creative applications, choose a Mac which can accommodate at least 4Gb of RAM. You might not need it now, but software requirements keep going up, and if you can't add more RAM later you could be stuck.

1.3 Hard disk size

The third big selling point of computers is the hard disk size. Where the RAM is for 'thinking space', the hard disk is for permanent storage.

Hard disk size is measured in Gb (gigabytes) and the basic Mac Mini comes with a 320Gb hard disk, while the top iMac has a 1Tb hard disk (terabyte = 1000 gigabytes), but it can be ordered with a 2Tb drive too. Hard disk capacities have increase substantially in recent years, and they've needed to in order to keep pace with higher-resolution digital photos and movie files, for example, Portable Macs have smaller hard drives. The MacBook starts at 250Gb, while the ultra-slim MacBook Air has a 120Gb drive.

That's all very well, but how big a hard disk do you need? That will depend on what you use your computer for, but by the time you've installed a couple of extra programs, built up a photo collection and maybe stored some movie clips, copied your

CD collection into iTunes and accumulated a few months' worth of letters, homework assignments and other documents, you'll have taken a big chunk out of the storage space of a 250Gb drive.

Still, 250Gb is a good starting point, and it'll take some time to fill up a disk of this size. If you think you might need more space it's better to specify a larger-capacity drive when you buy, though it is possible to fit a larger drive later. It's also possible to increase your storage capacity by using external disk drives, though these don't operate quite as fast as the inbuilt ones.

The Mac Pro is a special case. It's a professional machine which means it must be versatile and expandable. It can accommodate more than one hard disk – in fact there are bays for up to four hard disks, and these can be used for extra storage space, or for data backups.

1.4 Getting started: the Mac Mini

Now that we've explained the three main specifications for computers, it's going to be easier to examine the individual Macs in the range and their suitability for particular jobs. And we'll start with the Mac Mini, the cheapest Mac of all.

This is unlike any other computer you'll see. It's smaller than you might imagine if you've only ever seen it in pictures, and in fact it's only about 50% larger than a CD case, though quite a lot thicker. Early versions were cheap and quite low-powered, but the latest generation is much faster and slimmer, though also more expensive, alas.

The Mac Mini is perfect for PC owners who are undecided about making the switch to the Mac. It's sold without a keyboard, mouse or monitor, but the idea is that you supply your own. You simply unplug the cables from your current PC and plug them into the Mac instead. There may be a couple of setup adjustments you need to make along the way, and you may need an adaptor for the monitor, but that's the extent of any technical difficulties. (You will also need a USB keyboard and mouse.)

This makes the Mac Mini cheap (compared to other Macs) and really easy to set up. It's supremely practical, too, because you'll no longer be banging your knees on a huge tower system under your desk – the Mac mini is small enough to squeeze on to even the most cramped and cluttered computer desk.

It's efficient, too. It uses the same kind of power-saving technologies you find in laptops, and in standby mode it consumes just 10W of power.

If you want to try a Mac but you're not sure about committing a lot of cash, the Mac Mini is the one to buy. It might look like a toy, but it's nothing of the sort – it's a real computer of considerable ability.

The Mac Mini is a 'starter' Mac for those who already have a keyboard, mouse and monitor. This is how it comes. You just put it on your desk and plug in your existing equipment – you may need an adaptor for the monitor, depending on the type. You can get an idea of the size from the CD/DVD slot on the front (photo: courtesy of Apple).

1.5 Family workhorse: the iMac

Good as it is, the Mac Mini is still a kind of stopgap for those who are undecided about committing fully to the Mac. The fact is that the iMac is a better all-round computer for a number of reasons.

The first is that it comes with faster processors and the option of fitting more RAM. It can also accommodate larger hard disks. Perhaps the main point, though, is that the computer hardware is built into the back of the monitor, so you get an extremely elegant computer which doesn't actually have a base unit at all.

Apple's monitors are very good. By the time you've bought one separately, and of comparable quality, to go with a Mac Mini, you're getting close to the cost of a basic iMac. Besides, the iMac comes with a mouse and keyboard as standard – the Mac Mini comes with neither.

The latest version of the iMac has a brushed aluminium finish and a slimline aluminium keyboard. It's a very stylish machine, and if you've got to have a computer in your living room, then you (or your partner) are going to want one that looks good.

iMacs come in different sizes. Their all-in-one design makes them perfect for home use, while the most powerful versions rival Mac Pros for professional use.

Many computer users will be unimpressed and will point instead to how much cheaper a comparable PC system is. It's perfectly true. You have to decide how much you value style over cost. But don't imagine that 'style' is all the iMac has to offer. The minimalist design isn't just to look good. It takes up less space, and uses far fewer cables. You get a much clearer, cleaner environment to work in.

This is why the iMac is the best Mac for home users. And don't worry that it doesn't have quite the power of the Mac Pro.

Whenever there's another, more expensive model further up in the range, it generates a kind of 'performance anxiety' that puts you off the cheaper one. Forget it. For most jobs, the Mac Pro will provide no discernible performance advantage, and Apple deliberately pitches them at the professional graphic design market rather than general users. Indeed, the top-end iMacs are worthy alternatives to low-end Mac Pros. There's no sharp dividing line – it's more like a broad area of crossover.

1.6 Creative professionals: Mac Pro

The Mac Pro is for those who must have both performance and expandability; users for whom even the fastest computer is still too slow, and who may require specialized computing hardware for their particular field.

The Mac Pro is the most powerful Mac of all, and comes in an aluminium tower case. You can open it up to add extra hard disks, upgrade the memory and install other custom hardware (photo: courtesy of Apple).

In addition to its fast quad-core processors (two are used in the top-end 8-core machines), the Mac Pro can be fitted with a maximum of 16Gb RAM and four hard disk drives. It's a big machine, but that's because it must have space inside for additional components, as required, and it must be easy to open up so that extra hardware can be fitted.

It's the sort of machine that might be chosen by professional photographers, videographers and designers, particularly those working in 3D design and animation. But unless you know for sure that you're going to need every ounce of power that modern computing technology (and a lot of cash!) can provide, it's probably overkill.

Author insight

Unless you know for sure that you need a Mac Pro, an iMac is plenty powerful enough. The chief advantage of the Mac Pro is its expandability, but unless you know you need 8-core processing and three disk drives, it's an expensive and bulky route to follow.

1.7 The portable MacBook

The MacBook makes an excellent portable computer, and while the 13″ display might sound small, it's actually perfectly fine (photo: courtesy of Apple).

The Macs we've looked at so far are all static desktop machines. Apple also makes two ranges of laptops: the MacBook and the MacBook Pro, plus a third, standalone machine called the

MacBook Air. As the names suggest, MacBooks and MacBook Pros are aimed at general users and professionals respectively.

At one time the MacBook was available in either white or black, but while the white version has the classically elegant look that Apple's become famous for, the black one looked like a rather hideous and overpriced copy of Windows laptops half the price. A superficial judgement, certainly, but many choose Macs for their looks, and the black MacBook has since been dropped.

MacBooks come with 13″ widescreen displays. That's smaller than the screen on any PC laptop, but you shouldn't be put off by this. Macs use high-resolution displays and, unless you have trouble reading small text, the screen on the MacBook is easily big enough. Besides, it allows a much slimmer design. Not only is the MacBook thin, it's short from front-to-back, too. When the display hinges back, you don't immediately shut out everyone else in the room, and you don't get that slightly unstable top-heaviness that can affect other laptops.

The basic model has a 2.4GHz Core 2 Duo processor, 2Gb RAM and a 250Gb hard disk drive. This is fine for most purposes, but if you can afford the extra it's worth going for more RAM (up to 4Gb) and a larger hard disk (up to 500Gb).

The MacBook Air is the ultimate portable Mac (photo: courtesy of Apple) except for the new iPad, of course, but that's another story.

The MacBook Air is a special case. This is an ultra-lightweight Mac less than 2cm thick when the lid's closed and which weighs just 1.36kg. It uses the same 13″ display as the ordinary MacBook, but the small size has meant compromises in other areas. The processor is slightly slower, it comes with 2Gb RAM only and a smaller

120Gb hard disk drive. It's also more expensive, but this and the slightly lower specs are the price you pay for the exceptionally slim, lightweight and portable design.

1.8 Professional portability: the MacBook Pro

Professional users may need a bigger screen and more RAM, and that's where the MacBook Pro comes in. There are three main models, distinguished by their screen size – the 13″, 15″ and the 17″. MacBook Pros have slightly faster processors than the standard MacBook, and they come with 4Gb RAM as standard, which can be upgraded to a maximum of 8Gb.

The MacBook Pro is Apple's professional laptop. It comes in a one-piece aluminium body with a 13″, 15″ or 17″ display (photo: courtesy of Apple).

If you just need a general-purpose personal computer, the standard MacBook will do the job perfectly. But if you're a designer, an artist, an animator or are involved in any kind of creative business, a MacBook Pro will be the better choice because the demands of the job and the software you use will be higher.

1.9 Invasion of the iPads

Apple's new iPad has really captured the imagination of the public and the industry alike. The concept of a touch-screen computing 'tablet' is nothing new and it has been tried a number of times before without much success.

What Apple has done, though, is produce a machine which is simple, elegant and straightforward. It's not like an ordinary computer. It's more basic, true, but in this case it's a strength not a weakness. People who might be put off by the complexity of a regular computer are falling in love with the iPad.

It actually has a lot in common with the iPhone, and iPhone applications will also run on the iPad, though you need the newer-generation of iPad-specific software to make the most of the larger screen.

You can use the iPad to surf the Internet and send and receive emails, just as you can with an ordinary computer. There are tens of thousands of low-cost programs you can browse through and download from Apple's 'apps store', and special versions of Apple's iLife and iWork programs designed specifically for the iPad.

Will iPads take over the world? They use a simpler version of the Mac operating system and specially-written software, but they've taken off in a very big way.

iPads come with three different storage levels and two types of connectivity. They use solid state storage rather than hard disks, and you can get 16Gb, 32Gb and 64Gb versions. This is less than a regular Mac, but the simplicity of the iPad and the tasks it's designed for mean that you don't need anything like the capacity of an ordinary computer. All iPads offer wireless connectivity, so you can connect to the Internet using your wireless router or access point at home or at the office, but there are 3GS versions (in all three storage capacities) which can also connect to phone networks.

There are no buttons or keys. Everything is done using the iPad's touch-screen interface, and this is what makes it so appealing for beginners and people who don't like computers.

Our advice? Unless you know for sure that you need the extra capacity or the 3GS connectivity, go for the cheapest 16Gb version. It's a whole new type of computer, and a whole new way of using them, so make sure you like it first!

Author insight

Should you get an iPad? Opinions are divided, and even your author can't make up his mind. They're brilliantly simple, even for people who hate computers. Yet they're also quite limited, and in ways which aren't immediately obvious. Besides, you really need a 'proper' Mac too, for backups, synchronization and other routine tasks.

1.10 Mac vs PC: time to stop arguing!

When you're shopping for a Mac it's likely you will encounter many arguments in the Mac versus PC debate, particularly if you're asking around to find out which one you ought to buy. It's rare to find people who have used both for long enough to form a proper opinion, and as a result you tend to get unbalanced and sometimes grossly distorted viewpoints.

The principal arguments against Macs from PC fans are broadly as follows:

▶ *They cost a lot more*
▶ *You don't get the same power as a PC at the same price*
▶ *They're only for designers and 'creatives'*
▶ *You can't get the software*

▶ *They're all style and no substance*
▶ *They're not as versatile as PCs.*

There is some truth in some of these arguments, but they also overlook the Mac's strengths.

First, it's difficult to compare the relative performance of Macs and PCs at the same price because they use different operating systems and different applications. Whatever test you use, someone will argue that it's been weighted towards one machine or the other. Broadly, though, PCs may give you faster processing at a specific price point. It's certainly true that you can buy good, fast, up-to-date PCs for less than the price of an iMac or a MacBook, say.

The next notion, though, that Macs are only for designers, is long out of date. The professional design community has long preferred Macs, that's true, but all along Apple's specialities have been innovation, elegance and ease of use. And nowhere is this more obvious than its latest suite of iLife and iWork applications. These are not only cheap (free, in the case of iLife), they are also exceptionally good. We all imagine that free or bundled software must be cheap, old or ineffective, but the Apple applications are none of these. What's more, they are all clearly part of the same family and work together and not just as separate applications.

This changes the cost equation, too. The software provided free with Macs is very much better than people imagine 'free' software to be.

This affects the other suggestion, that you 'can't get the software'. Well, given that Macs already come with iPhoto, iCal, iTunes, iDVD, iMovie, Garage Band, Mail and Safari, the question is how much more you actually need. All high-end design software is, as you'd expect given its reputation, available on the Mac, and if you want to use the Mac in business you can get iWork (just £71 in the UK) or the Mac version of Microsoft Office. Oh yes, there is a Mac version.

It is true that there aren't as many software packages for the Mac as there are the PC, and that you might have to buy via mail order because most computer retailers don't stock them. In practice, though, the major applications in specific fields are generally available for both computers, and the Mac has a good number of very exciting, very inventive programs that you can't get on the PC.

Besides, with the release of Leopard/Snow Leopard, if the worst comes to the worst you can always buy a copy of Windows and start up your Mac as a PC for those applications which don't come in Mac versions at all.

Can you get the software? Macs come with a large number of programs pre-installed, and are very well supported with pro-level 'creative' applications like the 'Aperture' photo management program (photo: courtesy of Apple).

Style-wise, it's true that Apple puts a great deal of effort into the design of both its computers and its software, and it seems reasonable to argue that money spent here could have been spent on reducing the price or increasing the features. It's an argument you could have about any consumer item. Would you rather have cheap clothes or nice ones? Exactly. You don't have to base your buying decisions on ruthless practicality. You are allowed to choose things you actually like.

Finally, there's the question of versatility. Yes – hands up – PCs are more versatile. They can do a wider range of things, use a wider range of software and can be expanded with a wider range of specialist hardware.

But this is not something that everyone wants to do or needs to. You might be advised to buy a PC just in case you need to do these things in the future, but will you? Really? It's like buying a van instead of a car just in case you need to carry something big one day.

Author insight

The idea that you can start up your Mac as a PC using Boot Camp is tempting, but you need a big hard disk to make it work, plus the know-how to add an extra partition and install Windows from scratch. To be honest, if you want a PC, it's got to be easier just to buy one. They don't cost a fortune these days, after all, and it saves having all your eggs in one basket.

TEST

1 *Which makes more difference; processor 'speed' or processor 'family'?*

2 *How much RAM does a Mac need for basic everyday tasks?*

3 *How many gigabytes in a terabyte?*

4 *You can keep your existing monitor, keyboard and mouse and simply replace your PC base unit with a Mac... but which one?*

5 *Which Mac has the computer and the monitor combined into a single unit?*

6 *How many 'cores' are there in the top Mac Pros?*

7 *Why would you choose a MacBook Pro over the regular MacBook?*

8 *What's different about the MacBook Air?*

9 *Does the iPad use the same software as other Macs?*

10 *Can a Mac run PC software?*

2

How Macs work

In this chapter you will learn:
- *how Macs start up*
- *about the items on the Desktop*
- *basic mouse skills*
- *about menus, windows and dialogs*
- *how to use the Dock*
- *how to open files and run programs*
- *how to use the Finder*
- *what to do if your Mac crashes*
- *about shutdown and sleep mode*

2.1 Starting up

Macs may seem very different from PCs, especially if you go by what you've heard, but in fact one computer is, at heart, very much like another. And this is certainly true of Macs and PCs, which start up in a very similar fashion.

1 When you press the power button, the Mac goes through a series of basic hardware checks to make sure everything's working properly. This is when you hear the characteristic Mac 'chime'.
2 The Mac now loads the operating system from the hard disk. This is standard practice for all computers – the operating system is what controls the user interface and how programs and accessories work alongside the computer hardware. On the Mac, the operating system is OS X, on the PC it's Windows.

3 Loading the operating system takes quite a few seconds, during which you'll see the Mac loading screen. When the OS has finished loading, the Mac will display the Desktop.

2.2 The Desktop

The Desktop on the Mac is just like a real desktop. You use it to arrange the items you're working on at the moment, and you can either leave them out (in which case their icons will still be on the Desktop the next time you start the Mac up), or file them neatly away in folders – just like using a filing cabinet or desk drawers in an office.

The Mac Desktop has two items that are always visible. One is the Macintosh HD icon which represents the hard disk inside the Mac. You can double-click this to display its contents. The other is the Dock at the bottom or the side of the screen. This has icons (buttons) for various programs installed on your Mac.

The Mac's Desktop has an icon for the hard disk (top right) and a 'dock' running along the bottom with icons which you can use to start programs or to switch between them.

Author insight

Some people leave everything on their desktop like a great big pile of junk and sort through it when they need things. Others pack it with icons arranged in neat, orderly rows. That's not what the Desktop is for! If you're not using something, put it away!

2.3 Basic mouse skills

Like PCs, Macs are controlled using a mouse. When you move the mouse, a pointer moves around on the screen. There are a series of mouse actions which are fundamental to controlling computers.

▶ *Clicking: you do this to select an object on the screen, press a button or open a menu (by clicking on its title). Just move the mouse pointer over the object, button or menu, and press the mouse button once. Strictly speaking, we should call this 'left-clicking', because some mice have two buttons, left and right. The Apple Mighty Mouse is a little different from PC mice because it only has one button (this does have two 'sides' but it's not always set up to use the right side).*

▶ *Double-clicking: to do this, click on an object twice in quick succession. This may take a little practice initially. If you get the gap between the clicks right, this double-click action launches an icon. If it's a program icon, it starts the program; if it's a file icon, it opens the file using the relevant program.*

▶ *Dragging: this is used to move objects around the screen. You move the mouse pointer over the object and press the button, but don't release it. Instead, you keep the button pressed as you move the mouse. The object is selected and follows the mouse pointer as you move it around the screen. You might do this to move a document from one folder to another, for example, or drag the title bar of a window to move it to a different position on the screen.*

▶ *Scrolling: this is where you use the wheel that many mice have on the top to scroll up and down through documents or web pages. The Apple Mighty Mouse has a little ball rather than a wheel, but it works in the same way. Windows also have scroll bars which you can use to move around the document too.*

▶ *Right-clicking: this is used to display shortcut or context menus relevant to the item you've clicked on. The alternative, for those using single-button mice or who can't get the hang of right-clicking, is to hold down the Mac's [Ctrl] key as you left-click. This has the same effect.*

Author insight

Once you've used a mouse with a scroll wheel, you'll never look back. But the ball on a Mighty Mouse can get clogged up, and you can't take it apart to clean it. The solution? Moisten the ball slightly, then turn the mouse upside down and rub the scroll ball on a sheet of paper. How does that work? No idea.

2.4 Menus, dialogs and windows

Menus are at the heart of most applications on the Mac, just as they are on the PC. A menu is a list of options which opens up when you click on the menu title. On the Mac, the menus run along the top of the screen in a menu bar, although some windows, dialogs and palettes have small pop-up menus too.

To open a menu, you click on its title with the mouse. Then you move the mouse down the menu list to find the command you need. (Some of these commands open out into 'submenus'.) As soon as you select a menu option by clicking on it, the menu closes.

Menus appear at the top of the screen. When you click the menu title, a vertical list of options appears below – you click on the one you want.

Some commands carry out an action straight away. Others call up dialogs with further choices. For example, if you select some text in Microsoft Word and choose a different font from the Font menu, it's applied to the text straight away. But if you use the File > Save As command (i.e. open the File menu and select Save As) the program needs more information before it can proceed, so it displays the Save dialog, where you choose a new name for the file and the location where you want it stored. To put it simply, when the Mac needs more information before it can proceed, it displays a dialog.

When the Mac needs more information from you before it can proceed, it displays a dialog.

The files you work on are displayed in windows. You can usually work on more than one file at once, and each will have its own window. These can be moved around the screen – you just drag the window's title bar which runs horizontally along the top. You can change the size of a window by dragging its bottom right-hand corner, and close a window by clicking the red button in the top left-hand corner. The yellow button next to it minimizes the window to the Dock without actually closing it, while the green button to the right of that optimizes the window size to fit the document you're working on.

The documents and other items you work on are shown in 'windows', which can be resized and moved around the screen.

A window won't necessarily be able to show the whole of a document, in which case you'll see a scrollbar running vertically down the right-hand side of the window with a blue bar which you can drag up and down to scroll up and down the document. The small grey button on top of a Mighty Mouse can be used for vertical scrolling too. Occasionally, the document may be too wide for the window, for example when you zoom in on a digital photo. Here, you'll see a horizontal scrollbar running across the bottom of the window. This works in the same way as the vertical scrollbar.

Many Mac applications use toolbars. These sometimes run horizontally across the top of the screen directly under the menu bar, but in most modern Mac applications they are at the top of the application window. They contain a mixture of buttons and drop-down menus designed to make common tasks easier to carry out, partly by making them more accessible and partly through using icons which make them easy to recognize.

Many applications use palettes. These are like floating toolbars (though they are rectangular in shape rather than narrow strips) that stay on the screen for as long as you need them. Palettes, can be closed, just like windows, using a button in the top left-hand corner and can, like windows, be moved around by dragging the title bar. Palettes make it easier to organize your screen space to suit your way of working.

Many programs use 'palettes' to make commonly-used tools more accessible. Palettes can be moved around the screen, like windows.

There are subtle but important differences between the ways Macs handle windows and how the PC does it. On the PC, document windows have their own menu bars; on the Mac, the menu bar is fixed to the top of the screen, not individual windows. And to close an application on the PC, you simply close the window; on the Mac, the application stays open until you use the 'Quit' menu command.

2.5 Using the Dock

The Dock is like a control console for your Mac. It runs along the bottom of the screen or the side – you can choose which by using the Dock panel in the Mac's System Preferences – and it has buttons for launching programs. It's very similar in function to the Taskbar on a Windows PC. When you install a new program on your Mac, its icon will often appear here, but you can add and remove programs to the Dock manually. The Dock can eventually become a little overcrowded, but you can clear away icons you don't need simply by dragging them off the Dock, whereupon they disappear in a little puff of smoke. This doesn't mean you can no longer use those applications. They can always be reached via the Applications folder on your hard disk.

The Dock has other icons besides these. At the far left is the Finder icon – you can click this to open a new Finder window. The Finder is the Mac's equivalent of Windows Explorer on a PC. You use it to find and organize your files.

Next to the Finder is the Dashboard icon. The Dashboard displays the Mac's collection of widgets. These are small programs for common basic tasks and include a Calculator, Dictionary and more. There are now thousands of widgets in circulation, and we look at these in more depth in Chapter 15.

Towards the right-hand end of the Dock you will find an icon for the Mac's System Preferences. These are equivalent to the Control Panel on a PC, and are used to adjust the display settings, configure different user accounts and more. We look at these in more detail in Chapter 18.

Finally, at the far right of the Dock is the Trash icon. This is like the Recycle Bin on a PC. You drag files and folders here when you want to get rid of them, but they don't actually get destroyed until you use the Empty Trash menu command, just in case you change your mind.

The latest versions of the Mac operating system, Leopard and Snow Leopard, have a slightly different-looking Dock which adds an icon for the new Time Machine feature, and separates out a smaller section with two new icons for Downloads and Documents. We'll examine these more fully in Chapter 4.

Author insight

If every application on your Mac has an icon on the Dock, it can get pretty crowded. It slows you down, too, because it takes you just a little longer to identify the application you need. You can get rid of icons for apps you don't use very often just by dragging them off the Dock – they'll still be available in the Applications folder.

2.6 Starting applications

You can start an application by clicking its icon in the Dock, whereupon it will either open the last document you were working on, or a new blank document, or ask you to choose the one you want to open, depending on how that particular program is set up. It's generally quicker, though, to find the document in the Finder (see section 2.7) and double-click it. The Mac knows which application is needed for that document and starts it automatically.

It's quite likely you'll have two or more applications running at the same time as you work, and it's important to know how to switch between them. There are two main ways of doing this. One is to click on a window belonging to the application you want to use (windows are stacked on the screen, and you can often see parts of the window you want underneath the current window), though this does require a little experience. The more reliable method is to look on the Dock for the icon of the application you want to switch to and click on it. That brings the application's open window(s) to the front.

2.7 Using the Finder

Before you can make much progress using different applications on
your Mac, though, you need to understand the Finder. This is like
any other application, except that it's running all the time the Mac
is on and it's really your Mac's control centre. The Finder is what
you use to organize your files into folders and to find them again
when you need them. If you're already used to how PCs work,
think of the Finder as the Mac version of Windows Explorer.

You can create a Finder window by clicking the Finder icon in the
Dock. The Finder window contains a Sidebar for quick access to
common locations and tools, and a window displaying the contents
of whatever folder or disk drive you select.

*The Finder window is used to examine the contents of your hard disk and its folders. On the left is a Sidebar
which offers quick access to common locations.*

For example, if you click on the Macintosh HD icon in the Sidebar,
the window will display the contents of the Mac's hard disk.
You can choose the way these are displayed using the buttons
running along the top of the Finder window. For example, you can

display them as icons, a list, in columns or in Cover Flow mode (see section 4.3).

Essentially, the Mac contains just two types of object: files and folders. Folders are simply containers for files or other folders. You use folders to organize your files in a way that makes sense to you, although the Mac takes charge of some of this organization straight away, with an Applications folder and a System folder for operating system files you would normally leave well alone.

In Icon view, you can open a folder to see its contents by double-clicking it. The Finder window then displays the contents of that folder. You keep double-clicking as you 'drill down' through your folder system to get to the files you want.

In List view, folders are identified by right-facing arrows. You can click on the arrow to 'expand' the folder and display its contents. This gives you a much clearer picture of the filing system on your Mac, and while it's a little more complicated to take in, most Mac users prefer it to Icon view. List view is very similar to Windows Explorer on the PC.

Column view works differently. Here, the Finder window is split vertically into columns. When you click on a folder, its contents are displayed in a column to the right; if you click on a folder in that column, its contents are displayed in another column to the right... and so on. It's a system that makes much more sense when you try it out than it does when someone else is trying to explain it! When you get used to it, you may find that Column view becomes your favourite.

2.8 Your Home folder

The Mac already has a basic filing system in place and it's up to you whether you use this or invent your own. This may depend on whether your Mac is going to be used by other people as well as you. Like PCs, Macs are designed with multiple users in mind. Each user has their own account, which means they have their own login name and a password. Now if you're the only user, you don't have to worry about this. The Mac will start up and run without bothering you with these details. It's only later on, if other family or office members need to use it, that you need to worry about the details of user accounts.

But the by-product of this is that each user has a Home on the Mac, even if there is only one user – you. You can see it if you select Macintosh HD in the Finder Sidebar and open the Users folder. There, you'll see a folder with your username and a little home icon. This folder contains a number of other subfolders for, amongst other things, Documents, Movies, Music and Pictures. These folders are where the Mac will store your word processor files, your movie projects, your iTunes songs and your iPhoto library. Some of these also show up in the Places section of the Finder sidebar so that you can access them more quickly.

Now you can set up your own folder system outside this Home if you want, but then you lose the ability to keep your files separate from other people's. What happens is that if another user has an account on that Mac, they will log on with their own username and password and they will get access only to their Home folder and not yours. By keeping your files within the Home folder, you also keep them private.

Of course, within the Documents folder you can still set up your own folders and subfolders to create a personalized filing system set up specifically for the way you like to work.

rodlawton

Each user on a Mac has their own private 'Home' folder for their documents, photos, music and other files.

2.9 Managing folders and files

To create a new folder:

1 Open the folder where you want to create it and choose the New Folder command from the File menu.
2 A new folder is created with the name 'untitled folder' already selected, ready for you to type in the name you want.

You can use the Finder for moving files and folders around, too, and this is generally easier if you open two Finder windows (use the New Finder Window command on the File menu).

1 Navigate to the folder or file you want to move in one window.
2 Use the other window to find the folder you want to move it to.
3 Drag the file or folder icon from one window to the other.

To delete a file or folder:

Drag its icon on to the Trash icon on the toolbar.

The Trash isn't emptied straight away, just in case you need to recover items you threw away accidentally. Eventually, though, the Trash will contain so many items that it takes up a significant proportion of your Mac's hard disk space. If you're sure you don't need any of the items in the Trash you can empty it permanently by using the Empty Trash command on the Finder menu.

The Trash on a Mac is like the Recycle Bin on a PC. You have to empty it from time to time.

2.10 Finding files

It's important to develop a logical filing system and not just leave files and folders lying around haphazardly. It's all too easy to save a file and then forget where you saved it because you weren't paying proper attention or because you couldn't be bothered to navigate to the correct folder in the program's 'Save' dialog.

It's also important to pick file and folder names which are logical and which you'll recognize later. This is second nature to seasoned computer users, but it can take a while to develop this kind of discipline and to work out a system that makes sense to you.

When you do have a logical filing system in place, you'll be able to find any file on your computer straight away, even if you have thousands of them. It's like having a properly-organized filing cabinet in an office.

Spotlight is the Mac's own search tool. It can find every reference to a word or phrase on your hard disk in moments.

But for those of us who don't have this kind of discipline, or those occasions when there isn't time to be tidy and methodical about your filing, the Mac can step in with some fast and powerful search tools.

If you take a look at the menu bar (in any application, not just the Finder) you'll see a magnifying glass icon right at the end. You click this to display the Mac's Spotlight feature. All you do is type in the name of the file you're looking for and the Mac will search its hard disk to locate it. Spotlight keeps an index of the hard disk's contents which is continually updated, so it can find your files really fast.

Author insight

Spotlight is very good at finding files you've mislaid on your computer, but if you develop some kind of filing system you'll probably find you hardly ever need it. Gadgets are no substitute for a bit of organization and self-discipline!

2.11 What if your Mac crashes?

Sometimes Macs crash. It happens to all computers, and even these days to some household appliances. The cause is often impossible to pin down and associated with some freak circumstance deep in the computer's internal processes. Crashes just happen. Usually they're confined to a single program, but they can affect the whole machine. The usual symptom is that the computer freezes. The mouse pointer may keep moving, but the program doesn't respond when you try to click on menus or buttons. You may also see a constantly spinning 'beachball' instead of a pointer – this is the indication that the computer is 'thinking'.

So if a program is frozen, how do you get out of it? There's a special key combination you can use – [**Alt**]–[**Command**]–[**Esc**] (this is just like [**Ctrl**]–[**Alt**]–[**Delete**] on a PC). This key combination calls up the Mac's Force Quit dialog. This lists all the programs currently running and, as often as not, the one that's crashed will be displayed in red.

To Force Quit an application, you select it from the list and press the Force Quit button at the bottom of the dialog. This will usually solve the problem, though it may be that the whole system has become unstable by now and you need to restart the Mac. You may need to restart to make the rogue application run properly again anyway.

Like all computers, the Mac may crash one day. The Force Quit dialog enables you to close the offending program and carry on working.

Author insight

If your Mac crashes and you have to restart it, or if it's just installed a software update, it may appear to 'hang' when it starts up. Don't panic. Go away, make a cup of tea and come back. In situations like these it does take the Mac a little time to clear up and sort its files out, and it's usually fine in the end.

2.12 Shutdown and sleep

When you've finished working on your Mac you'll need to switch it off, but to do this you need to use the Shut Down command on the Apple menu. It's the same with PCs – you can't just disconnect the power.

There is another alternative if you're likely to use the computer again within a few hours, and that is to put it into sleep mode instead. Sleep mode switches off the display and the disk drives but maintains the operating system and any applications running in their current state using a small trickle of power. When you 'wake' the Mac again, it's ready to pick up where you left off almost instantly. Apple recommends sleep mode if the Mac's going to be used again within 24 hours, but that you should shut down if it's likely to be longer.

With the MacBook and MacBook Pro laptops, closing the lid will put them into sleep mode, and the internal battery can power the sleep mode for many hours. For example, you could set up a series of documents and presentations in advance of a meeting, close the display, take a train to your client's offices and open up when you get there ready to make your pitch straight away.

TEST

1 *Do Mac mice have one button or two?*

2 *If you rather work with a single mouse button (this is how the Mac was originally designed), what do you in programs with context (right-click) menus?)*

3 *On a PC, a program's menus are displayed at the top of the program windows. What's the difference with the Mac?*

4 *How do you remove an unwanted application from the Dock?*

5 *What are widgets?*

6 *The Mac's Finder windows offers a choice of views. Which is closest to Windows Explorer on a PC?*

7 *Why use the Home folder? Why not just store your files where you like on the hard disk?*

8 *What do you do if you don't know where you saved a file?*

9 *Sometimes the application you're working in may crash or freeze. What do you do?*

10 *How do you put your MacBook to sleep?*

3

Plug-in devices

In this chapter you will learn:
- *what devices can plug into a Mac*
- *about USB 1.1, 2.0 and Firewire*
- *about laser and inkjet printers*
- *how to scan old photos*
- *how to transfer photos from a digital camera*
- *how to connect a camcorder*
- *about external hard drives and USB flash drives*

3.1 What devices work with a Mac?

While Macs use totally different and incompatible software to PCs, these days they can almost always use the same plug-in devices. These include printers, scanners, digital cameras, memory card readers, camcorders and plug-in hard drives and portable USB flash drives. This wasn't always the case. In years gone by, Macs used different connectors and were not particularly well supported by makers of devices. You had to make sure that any peripheral you bought was compatible with the Mac, and these might only be available from specialist retailers.

To this day, you may get some computer 'experts' insisting this is one of the failings of the Mac, but this notion is long out of date. When the USB interface arrived, Macs and PCs both had the same cable interface, making things much simpler for the makers. And the introduction of the translucent plastic iMac in the 1990s reinvented the Mac as a fun, lifestyle-friendly computer. Today, makers recognize that although Macs still might be in the minority, they represent an important slice of the market which can't be ignored. As a result, it's rare to find a plug-in device which isn't Mac-compatible, and even those whose packaging doesn't carry the 'Mac' icon will often work.

It's always best to check that printers have Mac software, for example, and scanners too, because these rely on special drivers which handle the communication between the device and the computer. (Even here, though, the Mac OS comes with built-in set of drivers for popular products.) But other peripherals like digital cameras, external hard disks and 'stick' drives work like generic storage devices. You plug them in, their icon appears on the desktop and you can just treat it like another drive.

Don't worry that you won't be able to find plug-in devices for your Mac, because as a rule just about anything you can plug into a PC will plug into a Mac too. If in doubt, check the box.

3.2 Types of connection

The USB connector has simplified the whole business of connecting peripherals to computers. Macs may come with two USB ports (MacBook), four (Mac Mini and iMac) or five (Mac Pro). If this isn't enough, you can connect a USB hub to a single USB port on the computer – each hub has its own USB ports for connection peripherals – usually four, but sometimes more.

Some devices draw their power from the USB connection, notably portable external hard disk drives, so if you're using a hub, make sure it's one that has its own power supply.

The original USB 1.1 standard has now been superseded by the much faster USB 2.0 standard, but there may still be some older USB 1.1 peripherals around, so do check the specs. This is important for devices which routinely transfer large amounts of data. USB 1.1 is all right for keyboards, mice and printers, but you need USB 2.0 for external hard disks, memory card readers and scanners. All the USB ports on modern Macs are USB 2.0.

But Macs may also come with one or more Firewire ports. Firewire was used by Macs for high-speed data transfer before USB 2.0 came along, and even now it's still used for some kinds of data transfer, notably for transferring movie footage from camcorders. On the camcorder, it may be called an 'iLink' connection. Firewire comes in two speeds. The original is 'Firewire 400', but there's a newer, faster 'Firewire 800' which is used by a few pro-level devices.

Most Mac owners will only ever use USB 2.0 devices, though, and maybe the Firewire interface occasionally for connecting camcorders.

Macs also sport another interface which looks like a phone cable socket but isn't. This is the Ethernet connector, which you use to connect the Mac to a network. But since modern Macs use wireless Airport communications, you can also connect to networks without cables (although cable connections are generally a little faster and more reliable).

3.3 Choosing a printer

Generally, the first peripheral most people need is a printer. These come in two main types: laser printers and inkjet printers.

Laser printers use dry toner which is applied to the paper using a drum, then sealed into the paper with heat. Laser printers are common in offices because they are cheap to run, require little maintenance and produce printouts which are dry to the touch straight away. It's possible to get colour lasers too, but these are more expensive both to buy and to run. These too are popular in offices for their speed and economy, but they're not suitable for high-quality photographic output.

Almost all printers work with Macs as well as PCs, but do check the box before you buy. An MFD (Multi-Function Device) can scan photos and act as a standalone copier too.

Inkjet printers use a different technology, squirting tiny droplets of ink on to the paper as the print head moves across the sheet. Inkjet printers are cheaper than lasers and produce much higher quality colour printout. This makes them ideal for home and light office use. The latest models produce superb photo print quality, even those not designed specifically for photo output.

Really, if you're buying a printer for domestic use, an inkjet is the only logical choice. And you don't have to pay much to get a really good one. The cost is actually in the inks, and heavy users will soon notice that replacement ink cartridges are not cheap. This is one of the drawbacks of inkjet printers – that, and the periodic maintenance they require to keep the ink flowing smoothly. This is carried out automatically by the printer at set intervals, but it means even more ink is used up, though printer maker HP has experimented with recirculating ink systems that return the ink used for maintenance back to the ink tank.

Printers remain popular, but another type of device is slowly taking over – the multi-function device or MFD. MFDs are printers and scanners combined. The scanner sits on the top and you lift the lid then place the items you want to scan face-down on the glass plate (the platen).

But because the printer and the scanner are combined, you can bypass the computer altogether if you want to. MFDs usually have a standalone copy feature which means you can copy documents without having to switch the computer on. It's like having a colour photocopier in your own house – very useful for keeping records of correspondence, legal forms or even recipes which you want to pass on.

Author insight

Get a multi-function device rather than a printer. They don't cost a lot more and even if you don't use them for scanning photos or documents, the fact that they work as a standalone copier makes them worth the extra on its own. How many times have you wanted to make a copy of an important letter or document, for example?

3.4 Scanning your old photos

Scanners are useful things to have, whether they're standalone devices or built into an MFD. They're especially useful if you have boxes of old prints which you want to digitize on your Mac to preserve them for the future, put them on a web page or repair and enhance them and print them out all over again.

And you don't need a particularly expensive scanner to do this. Most can scan at a level of quality far higher than the things you're scanning.

Resolution is the defining power of the scanner, and it's measured in DPI (dots per inch). Typically, even an inexpensive one will have a resolution of 2400dpi, where even a high-quality photographic print is unlikely to have more than 300dpi-worth of detail.

The situation changes if you've got negatives and slides rather than prints. Some scanners have transparency adaptors for scanning these, but the quality of the scans is often disappointing – the pictures don't look as sharp as they should. This is because negatives and slides are tiny and they're being enlarged considerably. The engineering and optical quality of normal scanners just isn't up to the job.

To get the best definition from slides and negatives you need to use a proper film scanner, and these work differently. With a regular scanner, you place the original face-down, flat on the scanning bed. Indeed, they're called flatbed scanners. With a film scanner, the slide or negative is fixed in a special holder which is drawn into the scanner during the scanning process. Film scanners are designed specifically for the job, and this shows in the quality of the results.

3.5 Connecting a digital camera

Digital cameras can either be connected to the Mac via a USB cable, or you can take out the memory card and insert it into a card reader to transfer photos.

Scanners are perfect for transferring older photos to your computer, but few of us these days shoot with film cameras any more, preferring to use digital cameras instead. Here, of course, there's no need to scan the pictures because they're digital files already. It's still necessary, however, to find some way of transferring them from the camera to the computer, and there are two ways of doing this.

The first is to connect the camera to the computer using the USB cable included with the camera. If you installed the software that came with the camera, this may start up automatically and offer to copy across the photos automatically. Otherwise, you should find that the camera's icon appears on the Desktop, and that you can double-click it to open it and drag the photos across yourself using the Finder.

3.6 Using a memory card reader

For many people, a memory card reader will be more convenient than connecting the camera to the computer by cable. Here, you take the memory card out of the camera and plug it into a slot on the card reader (the card reader is connected to the computer). The memory card will appear on the Mac's Desktop and you can double-click it to open it in the Finder and copy files across.

Of course, what complicates things with memory cards is that there are a number of different formats. SD cards are the most common, and are found in the majority of compact digital cameras and some of the cheaper digital SLRs. Compact Flash cards are larger, and although they were once the most popular type, they're now found mainly in professional digital cameras.

These are the two most common types, though some Olympus and Fujifilm cameras use tiny xD cards, while Sony cameras usually use proprietary Memory Sticks.

This means you need to check you're buying the right kind of card reader for your camera's memory cards. The alternative is to buy a card reader with slots for all the main formats. These don't necessarily cost much more, and they give you more flexibility in the future if you decide to change cameras.

3.7 Movies from your camcorder

Compact digital cameras can also shoot movie clips, and this is an area where they have improved almost beyond recognition in the past couple of years, to the extent where many cameras can now shoot high-quality HD video, and some digital SLRs and hybrid cameras offer the kind of manual control over exposure and focus and lens choice that was once the province of only the most expensive professional camcorders.

At this rate, the days of the traditional camcorder do look numbered, though there have been developments here, too, towards solid-state storage (memory cards and hard disks) rather than tape, HD video (in the more expensive models) and smaller dimensions.

The good news is that you can get footage onto your Mac for playback and editing from almost any digital camcorder, cutting and editing clips, splicing them digitally and adding professional-looking transitions, fades, titles and credits.

That's exactly what iMovie is for. We won't get into a detailed explanation of what iMovie does here because it's covered more fully in Chapter 11. However, we will explain how the movies get from the camcorder to the computer. It's done via the Firewire, or iLink connector on the camcorder and the Firewire port on the Mac. You can use iMovie, which comes with all Macs as part of the iLife suite, to control the camera playback from the computer, stopping and starting the tape, and recording clips to the Mac's hard disk.

Apple does publish a list of camcorders which are officially compatible with iMovie on its website, but in practice there are many more which are not on that list which work fine. Indeed, any camcorder with a Firewire/iLink interface should just plug in and go.

More up-to-date solid state camcorders may connect via FireWire or USB, but the principle is the same – you import clips from the camcorder into iMovie and work on them from there.

You can transfer movies to your Mac too, using a FireWire (iLink) cable with older digital camcorders and USB cables or card readers with newer solid-state models.

Many camcorders and cameras save movies as individual files, and this makes things easier still. You can copy them across from the camera just as you would with a conventional digital photo and double-click them to play them back on the Mac, or import them into iMovie for editing.

Author insight

Do we need camcorders any more? The latest digital still cameras can also shoot very good quality movies, often in high definition. Real video buffs will still want a camcorder, but for video 'snapshots' a stills camera is perfect. Most also create simple, standalone movie files you can just copy across to your Mac.

3.8 Why external hard drives are useful

Printers, scanners, cameras and camcorders are probably the most obviously useful Mac accessories, but you should also consider investing in an external hard disk drive. Not the most glamorous of peripherals, to be sure, but one that's both practical and, occasionally, an absolute life-saver.

External hard drives come in different capacities and sizes. The largest will sit on your desk alongside your Mac and have their own power adaptor. They offer big capacities (500Gb, 1000Gb or more), but they're not portable.

Portable hard drives have smaller capacities (up to 500Gb currently), but apart from being smaller, they run on the power provided by the USB cable – they don't need a power cable at all. Portable drives are useful for all kinds of things. You can use them to boost the storage capacity of your Mac, you can use them for transporting large movie files or photo collections from one computer to another, and you can use them for possibly the most important function of all – backups.

Computer experts are always telling us to back up our important files, and they're right. Hard disks don't fail often, but they do fail. So just sit and think for a minute of the consequences of losing forever all the data on your computer – awful, isn't it? Backups are vital and, with a portable hard disk, easy to manage. Those who subscribe to a MobileMe account (see Chapter 14) get an Apple utility called Backup which makes it easy. Alternatively, if you're using Leopard or Snow Leopard (see Chapter 4), Time Machine will take care of it automatically and in the background with absolutely no effort on your part.

This is a portable external hard drive. It's small, neat, and simple to use (all you need to do is plug it in) but extremely useful for expanding your storage, transporting files or backing up your Mac.

Portability is an important factor. It's all very well having a static hard disk drive plugged into your computer, but if the computer is stolen or damaged in a fire, you can expect to lose your backup too. But with a portable drive, you can get into the routine of keeping it at a different location to your computer, and this is a key feature of any kind of backup strategy.

Author insight

Portable external hard drives are the best invention ever. They get their power from the USB cable, so they're clutter-free too. You can use them for transporting files, backups or simply increasing your Mac's storage capacity.

3.9 Portable USB drives

In the old days, the standard way of transferring files between computers was the floppy disk. It's been a long time since any Mac came equipped with a floppy disk drive, so how's it done now?

Usually, files these days are swapped over the Internet as email attachments or, for those working in an office, transferred over the office network. Sometimes, though, a simpler method is needed – when students need to take an assignment into class, maybe, or when amateur photographers want to take digital photos into a camera club meeting.

USB drives are perfect for transporting files. They're tiny enough to fit on a keyring but available in capacities up to a staggering 64Gb.

One way of doing this is to burn a CD. All modern Macs have built-in CD writers, and it's a comparatively simple process: you insert a blank CD, copy the files across to its icon and then burn it. This is a once-only process that writes the files permanently to the CD.

This takes a few moments to do, though, and it does seem quite wasteful, especially if the CD isn't filled, and if it's only being used for data transfer rather than permanent storage.

It's much better to use a solid-state USB drive, and these are widely available in computer and electronics stores. They have several advantages. For a start, they're quick and convenient to use. You plug them into a USB port on the Mac, their icon appears on the Desktop and you can just copy across the files you want to transfer using the Finder. They're also reusable – you can delete the information and copy across new files as many times as you like. They're very small and easy to carry around and can even be attached to keyrings. They're robust, there is no risk of physical scratches or marks affecting the data and nowadays they're pretty inexpensive, too. A 1Gb USB drive holds almost twice as much data as a CD, and you can get them in 2Gb, 4Gb right up to 64Gb.

These USB drives have become the new floppy!

Author insight

If you need Internet access but there's no convenient wireless access point, you can use a 'dongle'. Most of the big phone providers offer them on a contract or pay-as-you go basis. They plug into a USB port and connect to the provider's phone network, just like a mobile phone.

3.10 Keyboards and mice

Lastly, although most Macs are supplied with a keyboard and mouse, these are also available separately. This is especially relevant for the Mac Mini, which Apple has described as the

'BYODKM' computer (Bring Your Own Display, Keyboard and Mouse). The Mac Mini is designed as a taster for PC owners who want to try out a Mac without buying a whole system – you unhook the PC from these components and hook up the Mac Mini instead.

That's an extreme example, but there could be instances where you want to use a different keyboard, mouse or display with your Mac. These don't have to be Mac-specific. PC keyboards will work fine, though they do have to have a USB connection rather than the PS2 type (it may also be necessary to re-map certain control keys using the Mac's System Preferences). PC mice work fine, just as they are, even those with scroll wheels, and you can plug in a PC's display, too, though if it's an analogue rather than a digital display, you will need an adaptor for the Mac, which only has a digital connector.

Some laptop users prefer to use a plug-in USB keyboard rather than the built-in keyboards when they can because the keys are generally better. And a proper mouse is certainly preferable to a trackpad.

Apple's Magic Mouse is especially interesting, though it is expensive too at £50 in the UK. It uses the built-in Bluetooth capability of all current Macs to work without cables, and it has a unique one-piece top surface which can act as a single or a twin mouse button and also supports multi-directional scrolling with no moving parts. (The scroll ball in the conventional Mac mouse can pick up gunk and fluff.)

Not all devices connect by cable. Apple's Magic Mouse uses a wireless Bluetooth connection, and it's possible to swap data between Macs and some mobile phones this way, too.

All this should serve to emphasize the point made at the beginning of this chapter. These days the Mac is a mainstream computer that's catered for by nearly all peripherals makers as a matter of course, and this includes printers, scanners, cameras, disk drives and just about any other gadget you might want to get. If in doubt, just check the box for the 'Mac' icon or read the system requirements to see if the Mac is mentioned.

Note that this applies to hardware devices only and NOT to software!

Author insight

You don't have to use an Apple mouse with your Mac. You can use an ordinary PC mouse too without any special configuration processes or software drivers. Just plug it in to a USB port, and off you go.

TEST

1 *Macs and PCs both use USB connectors, but does that guarantee that all USB devices will work on the Mac?*

2 *What's the difference between USB and FireWire?*

3 *Macs can connect to Ethernet networks in two ways. What are they?*

4 *Laser printers are popular in offices but inkjets are better for home use. Why?*

5 *Can you connect a tape-based digital camcorder to your Mac?*

6 *Where does a portable external hard drive get its power?*

7 *What's the name of the backup tool in the latest versions of the Mac OS, Leopard and Snow Leopard?*

8 *Macs don't have floppy disk drives for transferring files, so what can you use instead?*

9 *You can use PC keyboards with a Mac, but what sort?*

10 *Can you name Apple's unique wireless mouse, and what's special about it?*

4

Leopard and Snow Leopard

In this chapter you will learn:
- *about Leopard and its replacement, Snow Leopard*
- *how Stacks work*
- *how Smart Folders can find files*
- *about Cover Flow and Quick Look*
- *how Spaces can help you work on many things at once*
- *how Time Machine can back up your data automatically*
- *about changes to the email, browsing and chat programs*
- *how Expose works and how to restore files in the Trash*

4.1 Which OS do you have?

Snow Leopard, or OS X 10.6 to give it its technical name,
is the latest version of the Mac operating system, and it replaces
OS X 10.5 Leopard, and OS X 10.4 Tiger before it, in much the
same way that Windows 7 has superseded Windows Vista and
Windows XP before it.

The jumps between Tiger and Leopard and Snow Leopard have
brought many important new features and improvements, but they
have not really changed the basic Mac experience. If you're using
a Mac that's still running Tiger, you should consider upgrading to
Snow Leopard, but it's not essential unless you want to use tools or
software which require it.

If your Mac came with Leopard, again it's worth considering
upgrading, but there's probably no pressing need to do so right now.

If you've just bought a Mac, it will have Snow Leopard installed already.

Mac OS X 10.6 Snow Leopard is the latest version of the Mac operating system and is pre-installed on all new Macs. It looks very similar to OS X 10.5 Leopard, but there have been some important change (photo: courtesy of Apple).

The difficulty with a book like this is catering for users with machines of different ages, and we've tried to keep it as general as possible. In this chapter, then, we're picking out the special features in Leopard and Snow Leopard that might make existing users want to upgrade. If you already have Snow Leopard, you can use this chapter to explore some of its special features in more detail.

A great deal of work has been done to the Mac operating system at a low level, behind the scenes, and this applies particularly in the swap from Leopard to Snow Leopard. The new version is faster and supports 64-bit processing (useful with very high-powered applications and key to future developments).

Some of the enhancements in Leopard and Snow Leopard apply to Safari, Mail and other Apple programs included as standard with Macs, but most apply to the Finder, and these are what we'll be looking at in this chapter.

4.2 Stacks

The Dock in Leopard has a new translucent look, and there's a
section over on the far right where you'll find a feature called Stacks.
Stacks in Leopard open in a fan shape to show you their contents.
By default, there's a Downloads Stack which opens to show recently
downloaded files. These are files you may have clicked on a web page,
or files which have been sent to you as email attachments which you
save. These open as an arcing list, or 'Fan' with a link to the original
Finder folder at the top. When there are too many files to display in a
Stack, it changes to show them in a window as a grid instead.

You can also add your own folders to this area of the Dock simply
by dragging them on to the Dock from the Finder. For example, you
can drag the Applications folder here, or your Documents folder.

The Stacks feature in Leopard does
have a weakness, though. It's no
use for accessing folders within
folders, and many applications
do indeed install into subfolders
within the Applications folder.
This applies even more to the
Documents folder, where you'll
almost certainly store your work
in subfolders.

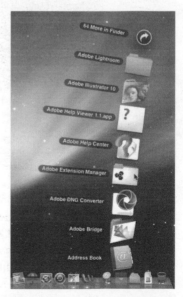

In Snow Leopard, though, Stacks
have been modified in such a way
that they're now much more useful.
You can choose whether they're
displayed in the Fan or Grid view,
but there's now a List option
which displays them as folders and
subfolders – it's just like using the
Finder in List view, in fact. Now
you can use the Dock to display

*Stacks can be used to show the contents of
favourite folders as a fan. It looks clever, but its
value is less certain – it's not much use if any of
the contents are in subfolders.*

your favourite folders and drill down through any subfolders to get to the items you want.

You may find Stacks very useful, but it's equally likely that you'll find them a novelty and not much more, especially if you're used to Macs already and you've managed perfectly well without them until now.

4.3 Cover Flow

Cover Flow was introduced with Leopard, and it's a new way to look at the contents of your folders. You can flick through your files, which are shown as large preview images.

Cover Flow is a new way to view the contents of folders in addition to the existing Icon, List and Column views. Anyone who's used the latest version of iTunes on a Mac may already have seen Cover Flow in action – visually, it's like flicking through a stack of CD covers. In Leopard and Snow Leopard that idea's been extended to the Finder, so that you can flick through a folder full of photos, for example, seeing each one move to the foreground as you drag the scrollbar underneath from left to right.

This is certainly a new way to browse through your files visually – something that's been lacking in the Mac OS until now. For those new to the Mac it's both novel and rather clever. For those who've been using Macs for a while, it may be less appealing because it is as much a cosmetic benefit as a practical one.

It's possible too that Apple is simply introducing consistency across its range of applications and devices. Both iTunes and the iPhone rely on Cover Flow, so it might look odd if the Mac OS didn't offer it too.

4.4 Finder Sidebar

For those used to OS X 10.4 Tiger and older versions of the Mac operating system, there are some changes in the Finder sidebar. It still offers quick access to items on your Mac, but the layout and functions are different.

In Tiger, the Sidebar was split into two sections. The top section listed Volumes attached to the Mac, including its hard disk(s), iDisk (for those with a MobileMe account – see section 14.2) and any computers currently connected via a network. In the bottom part were shortcuts to many locations on the hard disk, including standard items like the Desktop, the Applications folder, Documents, Movies, Music and Pictures. You were also able to add your own items to the bottom of the list simply by dragging files or folders on to the sidebar from the Finder.

The Finder sidebar offers quick access to items on your hard disk, any plug-in disk drives and other computers on the network.

In Leopard and Snow Leopard, the sidebar has more sections. These are: Devices,

Shared, Places, Search For. Devices is like the top section in the old sidebar, listing any disk drives built into or connected to the Mac. Any networked machines are now split off from this list and displayed in the Places section underneath. Note that with Leopard you no longer have to go looking for networked machines to connect to them manually – Leopard automatically scans for other machines on the network and lists them here. The Places section corresponds to the lower section in the Tiger sidebar. Here you'll find Applications, Desktop, Document and so on as before, together with any items you drag onto the sidebar yourself.

This all sounds quite complicated, but to start with, just think of the sidebar as a set of shortcuts to useful things on your Mac.

The Search For section is very interesting, though, and includes a new Leopard/Snow Leopard feature called Smart Folders.

Author insight

The Finder's sidebar is a great place to store files and folders you need often. All you have to do is drag them to the sidebar to add their icon. You're not moving the files and folders themselves, just creating a shortcut. And if you decide you don't need it any more, just drag it off the sidebar to remove it.

4.5 Smart Folders

If you've spent any time in iPhoto you may already know how Smart Albums work, and Smart Folders work on the same principle. You can think of them as saved searches. Let's imagine your hard disk is getting filled up by large image files. With a Smart Folder it'll be easy enough to track them down:

1 Open the **File** menu and choose **New Smart Folder**. A search window opens with a search bar prompting you to choose between searching the whole Mac or just your home folder, and between searching file contents or filenames. We want

to search the whole Mac, but we don't need to search the contents because we're not looking for text information.

2 To add our search criteria, click the '+' button at the far right of the search bar. This adds another bar with buttons for **Kind** and **Any**. Both of these are actually pop-up menus with different values, but we can leave **Kind** as it is and just open the **Any** menu. From this list we choose **Images**. Now our Smart Folder is locating all the image files on our Mac.

3 This can now be refined. Because of the options we've chosen, a third button appears on the search bar – **All**. This means the

Smart Folder will find all images of all types. If we want to, we can choose a specific type from this menu, for example **JPEG** or **TIFF**. What we're more interested in, though, is the file size, so we'll leave this set to **All**.

4 To look for specific file sizes, we need another search criterion, and we can create one by clicking the '+' button at the end of the search bar again. This time, from the first pop-up menu we choose **Size**. (If this doesn't appear on the list, click the **Other** option at the bottom.)

5 In the next pop-up to the right we choose '**greater than**', and in the box to the right of this we can type a number for the file size. Let's say we want to find files bigger than 10Mb. We type '**10**' and make sure the pop-up to the right is set to '**Mb**'.

6 As you choose the search options, the window below fills up with a list of matching files – the list will grow shorter as you refine the search criteria. You can check this list to make sure the search is finding the files you meant it to and, if it is, click the **Save** button at the top right to choose a name for your new Smart Search and to save it. It will now appear at the bottom of the **Search For** section of the sidebar, ready to be used any time you need to perform a clean-out of your big image files.

4.6 Quick Look

For a while Windows has scored over the Mac OS in its ability to display documents, particularly photos, as thumbnail images. You can open a folder full of photos and see what they are without having to rely solely on their filename to identify them.

Author insight

Quick Look is brilliant. It's one of those features you can't really see the point of at first, but then within about a week you can't do without it! Want to see what's in that Word document? Select it and hit the spacebar. You can even scroll down through the pages. Quick Look can display nearly all everyday document types.

Leopard puts that right with a feature called Quick Look, which works alongside Cover Flow in giving a visual representation of the contents of each file. In Leopard, when you view folder contents as icons, or use Cover Flow, files are displayed as thumbnail images showing the actual file contents. Leopard supports many file types, including Microsoft Office documents, PDF files and more.

With the new Quick Look feature, you can examine many different types of file without having to open them in an application.

But with Cover Flow, you're not limited to these previews. If you select a file in the Finder and hit the spacebar, Leopard displays a large-size preview in a pop-up window. Still not big enough? Then click the Full Screen button. When you've seen enough, you click the X button to close the window.

4.7 Spaces

Leopard makes it easy to view the contents of individual files without opening them, which is a real time-saver. But it also offers new ways to manage your windows and make the most of your screen space. It's called Spaces, and it's like being able to switch between four (or more) different monitors, depending on what you want to work on.

1 To activate Spaces you have to open the **System Preferences** and choose **Exposé & Spaces**. Select the **Spaces** tab and check the **Enable Spaces** box. By default, there are four Spaces, but you can add more if you think you'll need them. At the

bottom of the dialog is a list of the keyboard shortcuts you need – [F8] to display the Spaces, and arrow and number keys to move between them.

2 When you close the **System Preferences,** you'll be back where you were on the Mac, but with a difference. Now, when you hit [F8] a grid will pop-up showing the Spaces currently running. At the moment, only the top left space will have anything in it. If you click one of the others you'll get a blank Desktop as if you had no programs running at all.

3 You can now start opening files and applications in this Space, and return to the first one at any time by pressing [F8] and selecting it.

So what's the point? Let's imagine you're doing several things at once throughout the day (as most of us are). You can start Mail, Safari and iCal in one Space to handle your everyday admin, start up Pages and Keynote in another to work on a report or a business presentation, and start up iPhoto in a third Space to sort through your latest batch of digital photos when you take a coffee break from work.

Now running all these applications at once, in a single Space, will make your Desktop very cluttered. But by splitting them into different Spaces you give yourself a much cleaner, less cluttered working environment that can be organized according to the activity you're carrying out at any one time. You can also use Spaces to work on more than one project at once, and have Mail, Safari, iCal and so on open in both of them. The possibilities are endless.

Author insight

The Spaces feature can actually be very useful. Most of us run several applications at once and this can make your working environment very messy. But with Spaces, you can have your email program and iTunes running in one Space, say, and your work documents in another. Switching Spaces is a lot simpler than digging around through layers of windows.

4.8 Time Machine

Time Machine is one of Leopard's most impressive and most ambitious features. It's a tool for backing up the entire contents of your hard disk, automatically, in the background, for ever.

At a presentation shortly after the launch of Leopard, Apple revealed results of a survey they had conducted into backups. Over 90% of those they questioned said they considered backups vital, but only 4% of them actually did back up their files.

Traditionally, backup software has been time-consuming, technical and tricky to use, and Time Machine aims to sweep all this aside with a solution so simple that there's now no excuse for not backing up.

First, you need to invest in an external disk drive larger than the one in the Mac – preferably, several times larger. That's not as outlandish as it sounds because external USB hard disks are inexpensive these days, and a 500Gb drive will cost less than £50 in the UK, and a 1000Mb (terabyte) drive as little as £70–80.

The first time you plug in a new external drive, Leopard will ask you if you want to use it for Time Machine. It's best to use one drive specifically for this alone. Leopard will then perform a full backup, which will take some time, but will happen in the background, so you can get on with your work. Once this full backup has been made, Time Machine will carry out regular incremental backups, backing up only those things which have changed since last time.

If you need to restore your whole Mac to an earlier state, you can now restore that state with Time Machine, going back in time through its backups to find the state you want. You can also restore individual files and folders in the same way.

Apple describes Time Machine rather amusingly as 'a giant step backwards'. It's Leopard's innovative and supremely simple new backup tool.

Eventually, this external drive will fill up because Time Machine is adding more and more backups all the time. So what do you do then? Apple's suggestion is simple. Disconnect the drive, put it somewhere safe, get another drive and start again. It might not be the cheapest solution, but it's by far the simplest and most practical.

Time Machine has been enhanced in Snow Leopard to provide faster performance, especially for the initial backup.

For best security, you should unplug your external hard drive and store it away from your Mac between sessions.

Author insight

Everyone needs to keep their computer backed up, and almost no-one does. Yet with Time Machine it's so easy there's no excuse. Just plug in an external disk drive, activate Time Machine and the Mac does the rest. Don't ask, just do it!

4.9 Boot Camp

Boot Camp is not brand new, but Leopard was the first version of the Mac OS where it's been included as standard (previously it was an unfinished beta version which had to be downloaded from the Apple website). Boot Camp takes advantage of the fact that modern Macs use the same Intel processor family as Windows PCs and that, technically, there's no reason why Macs shouldn't run Windows.

Boot Camp enables the Mac to start as a PC, but it's important to understand that you will have to buy and install your own copy of Windows – Windows is not included with Boot Camp. You will also have to set up a separate disk partition for Windows to run in. The Boot Camp Assistant walks you through the whole process, and from this point on you can start your Mac up as a PC or a Mac, whichever you choose.

What you can't do, though, is run both at the same time (though there are utilities around to do this). But it does mean you can switch to PC mode for those occasions where you just don't have the software you need on the Mac.

4.10 Application enhancements

In addition to the changes to Finder, there are numerous enhancements to many of the Apple programs that come with the Mac OS. Some of the key changes are summarized here.

MAIL

Mail, the Mac's email program, was upgraded with several new features in Leopard. You can now set up Smart Mailboxes which work like Smart Folders in the Finder – once you've set up the search criteria, these mailboxes automatically display messages which match them. For example, you could have a Smart Mailbox set up to display messages containing any mention of your favourite soccer team.

And when you receive a message from someone who includes their telephone number and/or address, Mail will spot it and display a pop-up menu alongside which enables you to add the person to your Address Book as a new contact or amend the existing details if they're in it already.

Apple Mail now includes To Dos, Notes and Smart Mailboxes which can gather mail about specific subjects automatically.

There are stationery templates to make your messages look much more attractive and interesting. Perhaps the most useful additions, though, are the Notes and To Do features. Now, within Mail, you can jot down a telephone number, travel directions or any other information as a note and these appear in the Reminders section of Mail's new sidebar.

It's the same with To Dos. According to Apple, many users send themselves emails as reminders, so it made sense to incorporate this into Mail properly. The cleverest part is that these To Dos integrate with iCal, so that jobs you add in iCal also appear in Mail and vice versa.

In Snow Leopard, Apple has added compatibility with Microsoft Exchange, so it should now be possible to integrate Macs more effectively with company email systems.

SAFARI

Safari is the Mac's web browser and it received some subtle but useful enhancements in Leopard. Previously, the ability to open many web pages in tabs in the same window was one of Safari's top features, but now these tabs can be re-organized into a different order, turned into a new window or, if your screen is cluttered up with enough Safari windows already, you can combine them into a single window with multiple tabs. (For more on this, see section 5.6.)

Other improvements include a new Find function which opens a special Find bar at the top of the window. (This is not the same as searching the Web using a site like Google – it's for searching the text in the current web page.) When you search for a word or phrase, the Search bar tells you how many matches have been found and lets you go through them one by one using arrow buttons. The web page itself is dimmed out and the found items are highlighted so that you can easily see where they are. It's a huge improvement on traditional web page Find functions.

Safari is developed constantly and goes through its own update cycles independently of the Mac OS. At the time of writing, it's up to version 5.0. You don't have to use Safari, though, since Firefox and Google Chrome work equally well.

Safari has a Find tool which tells you how many matches it finds on a page and even highlights them for you.

ICHAT

If you're an Internet chat fan you'll be interested in the new features in Leopard's iChat application. It can be used as a text-only chat tool, but it really comes into its own when both you and your chat buddies are using computers with webcams (these are built into the monitor frame on many Mac models).

Some of the enhancements are purely cosmetic, like the ability to use a photo backdrop so that it looks as though you are standing in front of the Eiffel Tower or Niagara Falls or wherever, and the selection of weird distortions and other photo effects you can now apply to your video image.

The cleverest thing, though, is the way you can show your chat buddies keynote presentations (for example) live. In fact, this can be done with a wide range of applications. Your video image shrinks down to a corner of the screen, but you can still keep up a video commentary on what you're showing on the screen. It's really quite remarkable to be able to do this, and simple to set up, too.

For those who use chat programs, iChat will be a revelation, and its theatre mode lets you show other people things on your computer.

In Snow Leopard, iChat has been improved, with higher resolution and better all-round reliability. It's really designed for communication between Mac users running iChat, though, and the video options with other chat services may be limited.

Author insight

iChat is very good, but it doesn't support MSN, which is a pity since that looks like the most popular chat service at the moment. There is an MSN chat program for the Mac which you can get from Microsoft (it also comes with Microsoft Office), but it doesn't have the same capabilities as iChat.

4.11 Expose and the Trash

If you used System Preferences to experiment with the Mac's Spaces feature, you'll have noticed the Expose tab. Expose is a system for displaying the contents of all open application windows by moving the mouse pointer towards a corner of the screen. It works well enough, but you can get by perfectly well without it.

In Snow Leopard, though, Expose has been integrated with the Dock, so that you can use it in the original way, but you can also click and hold on an application icon in the Dock to display any windows open in that application. You can then release the mouse and click on the window you want.

And there's been a small but significant change to the Trash in Snow Leopard. Previously, you could double-click the Trash to open it and drag out any folders or files you've decided to keep, just as you'd expect. Now, though, you have the option of 'restoring' them to their original location, just as you can with a PC.

TEST

1 *Where can you find 'stacks', and what are the three display options in Snow Leopard?*

2 *What is 'Cover Flow'?*

3 *If you connect a hard disk or a USB stick to your Mac, its icon will appear on the Desktop... but where else?*

4 *What do Smart Folders do?*

5 *How do you see what's in a file without actually opening it?*

6 *Leopard and Snow Leopard have a feature to help you if you're working on two or more distinct activities at the same time – what is it?*

7 *The Mac has a tool for carrying out automatic backups in the background. What's it called, and what else will you need?*

8 *Can a Mac run PC software?*

9 *What's the name of the Mac's web browser, and are there any alternatives?*

10 *What happens if you change your mind about deleting a file?*

5

···

Internet and email

In this chapter you will learn:
- *how dial-up and broadband connections differ*
- *about routers and modems*
- *about Safari*
- *how to use bookmarks*
- *how to shop online*
- *about tabbed browsing*
- *how to set up an email account*
- *how to send and receive mail*
- *what to do with 'junk'*

5.1 Getting online

To use the Internet and email with your Mac, you will need an Internet connection. In the old days this was achieved using a modem, a device which fitted between the computer and the phone line and converted the computer data into a signal the phone line could carry. Some Macs were supplied with modems built in. However, these dial-up connections via modems and regular phone lines are slow and impractical for the way the Internet is used today. Besides, they tie up the phone line while the computer is online, making voice calls impossible.

The modern way to connect to the Internet is via an ADSL or broadband connection. This has many advantages, including much faster data transfer rates, which are essential for things like video chat, downloading music or watching video clips on YouTube.

To use broadband in the UK you must first get your phone line converted. This is usually organized by the company you buy your broadband service from as part of the overall package. The work is done at the local exchange – you don't usually have an engineer calling at your house – and typically takes a few days.

Most broadband accounts come with a modem, but it's worth upgrading to a router, which can connect several computers to each other and the Internet.

You then need a device for connecting your computer to the phone line. This may be a broadband modem. These are often supplied free as part of your broadband subscription. Their disadvantage is that they can only connect one computer to the Internet.

The other option is a router. A router is a device designed to connect two or more computers to form a network, but many also incorporate a broadband modem. If you only have one computer, they work just like a broadband modem. But if you have two or more computers, you can connect each to this single router, and they will all be able to access the Internet through it. It will also be possible to swap files between these computers because they are now on a network.

A broadband router (also called an ADSL router or modem router) is the best way to connect to the Internet because it's the most flexible. And if you buy a wireless router, you will not need to connect your Mac to it with a cable. All new Macs come with Airport wireless networking as standard, so you will be able to use them to connect to the Internet anywhere in the house as long as it's within the router's wireless range.

Not only that, a router will provide an access point for other devices in the house too, including PCs, games consoles and some portable wireless devices like iPhones and iPads.

SETTING UP YOUR CONNECTION

There are two ways of setting up an Internet connection, depending on whether you're using a modem or a router. The company supplying your broadband connection will supply you with all the technical details needed to configure your connection, though these will only apply to any modem or router supplied by them. If you buy a router separately, you will need to use the same information in conjunction with the router's own manual.

Some broadband companies will supply instructions specifically for Mac users, though many assume you have a PC. If you're having any difficulties with the setup, try the Mac's Network Setup Assistant. You can find this by opening the System Preferences using the icon on the Dock and then clicking the Network button. At the bottom of the Network dialog is an Assist me button which launches the Assistant. This walks you through the configuration process step-by-step, and this is where you'll need the account and setup information provided by your broadband company.

If you're setting up a router, the process is slightly different. With a modem, it's the Mac that handles all the setup information. With a router, you program this into the router itself. The router instructions will tell you how to apply the settings, and many offer a wizard which walks you through the process step-by-step. Again, this is where you'll need the account information from your broadband company.

Setting up Internet accounts isn't at all difficult, but if you haven't done it before it can be confusing. With this in mind, you might want to choose a broadband provider which supports Mac owners as well as PC owners.

It's not the most cost-effective solution, but if your broadband supplier provides a modem, you can get started with that and then invest in a router later on to get the advantage of networking and wireless connections. Ideally, though, you should look for one that supplies a router as part of the package.

Many companies are now offering all-in-one phone, TV and broadband services. If you choose one of these you should find that the Internet connection is the same in principle, but that the hardware device supplied may be more complicated than a simple router or modem.

Your Internet provider will give you the information you need to configure your modem or router.

WORKING AWAY FROM HOME

One big advantage of wireless networking is that you can more easily work away from home. It's not always possible to find a convenient wireless hotspot, but it's becoming easier. For example, if you're visiting a business colleague or customer, they may have wireless access points within the office or the building that you can use directly, although most will require authorization in the form of a username and a password, for example. Friends and relatives will often have their own wireless routers too, and the Mac will identify these automatically and ask if you want to use them to connect to the Internet. If you're staying in a big hotel you'll usually find that Internet access is available, but that it's password-protected and there's a charge for using it. Smaller hotels, though, may have much less formal arrangements and may not make any charge for using their wireless connection. Just ask at the reception desk to find out. Some cafes offer Internet access, but again you have to pay a charge to use them, and you'll be on your third espresso by the time you've got past the registration screens. It may also be possible to pick up a stray wireless connection in the street, but it's very unwise to use networks you find without asking permission because it's a criminal offence to steal bandwidth from other people's networks in these circumstances, and arrests have been made on this basis.

5.2 Getting started with Safari

Once your Internet connection is configured, when you start Safari, it will connect to the Internet automatically. With old-fashioned dial-up connections, this might take 30 seconds or more, but today's broadband accounts are always on, so you should be online in seconds.

Safari will now load your home page. By default, this will be the Apple website, but you can change this to whatever you like by choosing Preferences from the Safari menu. In the General tab you will see a box for the Home page. Type in the address of the page you would like as your home page here.

There are three main ways of going to web pages in Safari. One is to follow links on other pages, another is to type the address of the web page into the Address Bar running along the top of the window, and a third way is to use a bookmark you've saved previously.

The same applies in other web browsers like Firefox or Google Chrome. The menus and the dialogs may look different, but browsers all work in much the same way.

Author insight

You don't have to use Safari as your web browser, even if it does come free with the Mac. Many people use FireFox instead, and Google Chrome is very good too. The neat thing about Google Chrome is that the address box doubles as the search box too.

5.3 Using bookmarks

Web addresses can be hard to remember and time-consuming to
type in, so bookmarks are the easy way to store the locations of
your favourite sites.

To create a bookmark:

1 Go to the page you want
   and choose **Add Bookmark**
   from the **Bookmarks** menu.
2 A dialog will pop up where
   you can choose a name for
   the bookmark and where
   you want to save it.
3 By default, Safari will
   display the web page title
   chosen by its designer,
   but you will often find it
   useful to type in something
   shorter and easier to
   recognize later.
4 As to where you save the
   bookmark, there are three
   choices. You can save it
   in the main bookmark list

with no attempt at organization, you can save it in a bookmark
folder (depending on whether you have any set up yet), or you
can save it in the Bookmark bar, which runs horizontally
across the top of the screen. This bar should be kept for
the pages you view most often, though, because the space
available is limited.

To view your bookmarks:

1 Click the **Show all bookmarks** button at the far left-hand end
   of the Bookmarks bar.

2 Using this window you can create new folders for organizing your bookmarks, and you can also choose which will be visible directly in the Bookmarks menu by dragging them to the Bookmarks menu collection. You can also change what's displayed in the Bookmarks bar collection, and hence the Bookmarks bar itself.

3 To visit any of the web pages in your list of bookmarks, just double-click it.

Different web browsers and different versions of Safari will handle bookmarks differently, so this is just a guide.

Author insight

You may need to clear out your browser's bookmarks periodically. They're very easy to add, and they quickly mount up, and the more you've got, the harder it gets to find the ones you really need.

5.4 Searching online

The Web, as we're constantly being reminded, contains an almost unimaginable wealth of information on any topic you could possibly think of. This is where you need to use a search engine. These search the whole Web for the words or phrases you enter in the search field and come back with a list of websites containing them. The trouble is that these may run to tens of thousands, and there is an awful lot of dross and irrelevant information out there which you need to sift through to find what you want. After a while you develop an eye for the sites which are going to be reliable and offer the most useful information, but it helps to use a good search engine in the first place, because the smarter ones can identify the most relevant sites and put them at the top of the list.

One of the best-known search engines today is Google. It's now so prominent that Safari includes a Google search box in the top right-hand corner of the toolbar:

1 First, type the word or phrase you're looking for onto the search box and press [**Return**].

2 Google will come back with a list of sites, together with an extract to help you identify those which may be most useful.

3 To view a website, just click on its title in the list of search results. Better still, [**Command**]-click it to open it in a new tab so that your search results remain accessible.

Google is not the only search engine you can use, though. For example, you could try Microsoft's new Bing service at www.bing.com. All you need to do is type the address into Safari's Address bar to go to the site.

5.5 Buying online

It's now possible to buy many items on the Web at lower prices than you could find elsewhere, and there are many more things you can buy online which are simply not available in ordinary stores.

Buying online may seem a little daunting at first because you're dealing with a machine and not a real person, and the transaction doesn't feel quite as concrete. You may also have heard scare stories about Internet fraud and goods which fail to arrive.

Buying online is easy, and can often be less error-prone than doing it by phone.

In reality, the risks are no greater than ordering by telephone or from a mail order catalogue. Think of it this way: when you order via a website you're telling a computer what you want; when you order by telephone, you're telling a human operator who's probably typing it into exactly the same computer…

It is best to stick to well-known brands or companies, especially those you've seen advertised in magazines or which you've been told about by friends. One very good example is www.amazon.co.uk, which sells books, DVDs, photographic equipment and more. A few years ago, comparatively few people had heard of Amazon and fewer still used it regularly. Now, it's one of the best-known online stores.

Online transactions are quite straightforward, and you get confirmation in writing straight away by email or via your web browser, which you don't get when ordering goods by phone.

Typically, this is how it works:

1   If it's the first time you've bought from this particular company, you'll usually be asked to create a personal account, with your own username and password so that no one else has access to it.
2   Browse the site for the items you want and add them to a virtual shopping trolley or basket.
3   When you've finished shopping you go to the checkout page, where you can check and confirm the contents of your basket. You'll be shown a total cost, plus any postage or packing charges.
4   The payment process usually takes place over a series of screens, step-by-step. You'll be asked for the details of the card which you're going to pay with, and then the address you want the goods delivered to. This will usually be the cardholder's home address – the card company may refuse to authorize the payment where delivery is to a different address, though this depends on the amount and the company.
5   Finally, you complete the checkout process and confirm your order. You'll have been asked for your email address at some point in the registration/checkout process, and confirmation of the order will now be sent to you. This is your permanent record of the transaction, and you can print it out if you wish, but it's stored on your computer anyway. Some websites may display the order confirmation as a web page instead, and you should print this out in the absence of any email confirmation.
6   Your goods will be delivered by post, just as if you'd ordered by phone or from a catalogue.

5.6 Working with tabs

Sometimes it's useful to have more than one web page open at a time, and there are two ways of doing this. One is to open up the new web page in a new window, and you can do this by using the New Window command on the File menu and typing the address into the new Safari window's Address bar.

Alternatively, if you're following a link from an existing page, you can hold down [Ctrl] as you click on the link. This displays a pop-up shortcut menu, and the first two options are Open Link in New Window and Open Link in New Tab.

When you use this second option, Safari creates a new tab within the current window, and loads that page into it. You can see all the open tabs in a horizontal bar which appears below the Bookmarks bar. (If you're using Tiger and you don't see any tabs, open the Safari Preferences, go to the Tabs section and make sure Enable Tabbed Browsing is switched on.)

See the row of tabs running across below Address bar? Each one holds a different web page. Click on the tab to view the page.

There's an even quicker way to open links in new tabs – just hold down [**Command**] as you click the link.

Tabs are a great way to browse through lots of linked pages because you don't fill up your screen with lots of separate windows, and you can keep the page you started from open, which means you're less likely to get lost on the Internet.

Author insight

All modern browsers, including Safari, support tabs, and these have to be one of the smartest ideas in browser design for years. They're really useful if you're reading a page with some potentially useful links. If you [**Command**]-click on a link, that page opens in a new tab, ready for a closer look later, but you stay on the current one.

5.7 Getting starting with Mail

Once your Internet connection is working there's nothing else you need to do in order to be able to surf the Web. With email, it's different. The Internet connection is only half the story – you also have to set up your email account(s) in Mail.

You normally get an email account as part of your broadband package, but it's also possible to set up free email accounts separately with Yahoo! and other providers.

To set up an email account:

1 Choose **Preferences** from the **Mail** menu and then click the **Accounts** button. This window will show you the email accounts currently set up, if any, and in the bottom left-hand corner is a '**+**' button for adding a new one.

2 Press this. Mail will start a step-by-step guide to adding an account, and for this you will need certain information from the company providing the email account.

3 First, you type in your name, your email address and your password. The email address and password will have been given to you when you set up the account.

Outgoing Mail Server

Description:	(optional)
Outgoing Mail Server:	smtp.freeserve.net
	☑ Use only this server
☐ Use Authentication	
User Name:	
Password:	

Cancel   Go Back   Continue

4 Next, in the **Incoming Mail Server** window, choose the account type from a menu. Most are POP accounts. This means the emails are downloaded from a computer called a POP server to your Mac. In this same window you need to type in a **Description** of your account (just so that you can recognize it from a list if necessary), the **Incoming Mail Server**, **User Name** and **Password**. This information will be provided by the email service provider. At this point, Mail will check this connection is working.

5 Next, specify the **Outgoing Mail Server**. Here, you should use the outgoing mail server specified by your broadband company. If you set up an email account with another provider, they may give you a different address to type in, but this probably won't work. Broadband providers are prickly about letting you sending mail through any other server than their own (we must presume there's a good technical reason for this). Don't check the **Use Authentication** box unless your email provider's told you to. Mail will now check this connection and, if all's well, you've successfully set up your email account.

Normally, email messages are stored on the mail server (or POP server) until you connect and download them to your computer. Similarly, any messages you write are stored on your computer until you send them. This is all very well, but it means you can only read your mail on one particular machine. Sometimes when you're away from home you might want to check your mail, so what do you do?

For this you need a web mail account. Here, the messages stay permanently on the mail server, and you read and reply to them using a regular web browser on any computer.

Does this mean you'll need two email addresses and you'll have to check for mail in two places? Possibly, though there's a lot of crossover these days. Yahoo! web mail accounts, for example, also have a regular POP server, so that you can view your mail online or have it downloaded automatically to your Mac. And most web mail services will also let you retrieve mail from your usual POP server so that you can get all your regular mail through a web browser – all you'll need is your username and password.

Author insight

Apple Mail is very good, but web-based email may be better. Google Mail is free, and entirely browser-based, so you can access it on any computer. The interface isn't as pretty, but it does much the same things as Apple Mail. (Actually, you can access your Google Mail using Apple Mail, too.)

5.8 Organizing your mail

Setting up email accounts might sound technical, but if you take a methodical approach using the information provided by the email service, it's not hard. And, you only have to do it once.

Once that's done, you'll find the Mail application as easy to figure out as other Mac software. On the left is a Sidebar listing your Inbox (where all new messages arrive), Reminders (see section 12.3), and a list of any folders you've set up on your Mac to keep your mail organized. When you click on any of these items, a list of messages they contain appears in the main window to the right.

Depending on how you've got the Mail display set up, you may also see a Preview window below this, so that when you click on a message, you can read its contents below. Otherwise, you just double-click on a message to view it in a new window.

The Mail Inbox is like the text message inbox on a mobile phone. However, where you might regularly delete text messages on your phone to save space, on the Mac there's no need to delete emails because they take up very little room compared with the size of the hard disk. Besides, you never know when you might need to refer to them much later. But while storage space isn't a problem, having an Inbox filling up with hundreds of messages most definitely is. Some messages can clearly be deleted (we'll look at junk mail and spam in a moment), but others need to be filed out of the way.

To do this, choose New Mailbox from the Mailbox menu (Mailbox is the name that Mail uses for an email folder). You can now drag messages out of the Inbox and into this new mailbox. Mailboxes can be organized just like folders in the Finder, so you can make your filing system as complicated (or as simple) as you like.

Mailboxes are folders for organizing and storing your messages, helping you to find them later. Here, we have a mailbox we've set up for News.

5.9 Sending and receiving mail

Sending an email is easy.

1 Click the New Message button on the toolbar at the top of the window. You'll need to type in who the message is to, a title for the message and, finally, in the main window, the message itself.

2 You will need to know the other person's email address, obviously, and you can type this directly into the To: box.

In practice, the sensible way of doing it is to add them to your Address Book instead – and you can open this by pressing the Address Book button on the toolbar. Why is this smarter? Because you can now just type their name (or nickname) into the To: box of your message, and Mail will automatically look them up in the Address Book and insert their email address for you. It's a lot easier to type (and to remember) a person's name than it is their email address.

3 To send a message, click the Send button on the toolbar to show the message window. When you type a name into the To: box, Mail will automatically look it up in the Mac's Address Book.

You don't need to do anything to receive emails – they arrive automatically because Mail checks for new messages at regular intervals. And if you want to reply to a message, you don't have to create a new message from scratch; instead, you can simply press the Reply button. Mail will automatically insert the other person's email address in your response.

There's a lot more to Mail than this, but you can explore it at your own pace using the online Help. There is one more thing you might like to know straight away, though – you can use Mail to send files to other people. You do this by typing the message and then pressing the Attach button on the message window's toolbar. This opens a dialog where you can locate the file you want to send on your hard disk.

One word of warning – check before sending files bigger than 5Mb or so, because the other person's email server may reject the attachment for being too large.

5.10 Dealing with junk mail

While email has undoubtedly changed the way we communicate, it's also opened the floodgates to countless get-rich-quick schemes, advertisements, online scams and ghastly 'enhancement' products (and if you don't know what that means, consider yourself lucky). Mail calls this 'junk' and is pretty good at recognizing it automatically, and diverting it to the special Junk folder in the Sidebar. The process isn't perfect, though, and it's a good idea to click on this folder now and again to check its contents. If you find a message that actually isn't junk, click on it to select it and press the Not Junk button on the toolbar. Similarly, if junk mail is still making it into your Inbox, select the offending message and press the Junk button to send it to the Junk folder.

Doing this helps to train Mail to recognize the junk you receive more reliably, so that after doing this for a few weeks you may find it's not making any more mistakes and that you don't need to check so often.

You should be especially wary of any emails which ask you to confirm or supply confidential user information or passwords. They may appear to be from known and respectable companies, like your bank or building society, for example, and may say that their database needs updating or even that there's been an attempt to access your account and that you need to re-enter your information – they can be very convincing.

This is called 'phishing', and it's a very common and dangerous kind of spam. Two things give it away: (1) the company logo may not look quite right, the email address it comes from may be suspicious and there may be grammar or spelling errors; (2) in reality, bona fide companies never ask you to confirm security information in this way. If in doubt, phone up the company concerned to see if they know anything about this email. You can be sure that if your bank or building society really did have any concerns they needed to speak to you about, they would call or write to you direct.

Author insight

Don't reply to junk messages. You won't be getting through to a human, but you will be confirming that your email address is 'live', and potentially attracting even more junk mail as a result.

TEST

1 What's the difference between a broadband 'modem' and a 'router'.

2 Are wireless connections free?

3 Is Safari the only web browser for Macs?

4 Google is probably the world's best-known search engine, but what's the name of the new rival 'decision engine' from Microsoft?

5 What are the two safeguards used by online shopping sites?

6 What do a browsers' 'tabs' do?

7 The Mac's Mail program is perfect for regular email accounts, but what if you want to be able to access your mail on any computer, wherever you are?

8 The Mail application can look up email addresses automatically when you enter the recipient's name using information stored in what other application?

9 How should you deal with junk mail?

10 What is 'phishing'?

6

....

Apple iWork

In this chapter you will learn:
* *what the iWork programs do*
* *how to write a letter and design a leaflet in Pages*
* *how to create presentations and charts in Keynote*
* *the principles of spreadsheets*
* *how Numbers is different*
* *how to swap files with Microsoft Office users*

6.1 What is iWork?

Macs are often thought of as creative or lifestyle computers, but they are actually very effective business tools too. Indeed, the world's best known office suite – Microsoft Office – is also available in a Mac version, and we'll be covering that in the next chapter. But Apple publishes its own, cheaper alternative to Microsoft Office. It's called iWork, and a 30-day trial version is included with new Macs.

iWork originally consisted of just two programs; a word-processor called Pages and a presentations program called Keynote. But when Apple launched iWork 08, apart from a host of changes to these core programs, it added a new program called Numbers. Now iWork offers the same trio of applications you get in Microsoft Office – a word processor, a spreadsheet and a presentations tool. What's more, the applications in iWork are arguably more user-friendly and look more modern, and are certainly packed with neat touches to help you get your work done more quickly.

Since then, iWork 09 has come out, and in the examples in this chapter we'll aim to cover both versions. The instructions will be for iWork 08, but we'll highlight any changes or new features in iWork 09.

Macs come with trial versions of the iWork applications, so you can try them out for nothing. If you like what you see, you can purchase the full suite for just £71 (UK price), and this makes iWork an amazing bargain in the light of what it can do.

iWork is Apple's equivalent of Microsoft Office. It consists of a word processor, spreadsheet and presentations program, and it's much more powerful than the price tag might suggest.

6.2 Writing a letter in Pages

We'll start by taking a look at Pages, which is a word processing program with a difference, in that you can start with a blank page as usual or choose a ready-made design template.

These are not like the templates you get in Microsoft Word. A Pages template doesn't consist of just one page, but many different page layouts, so that you can choose a different layout for each page as you build up your document.

For now, though, we'll start with something simpler – writing a letter. In previous version of Pages, no distinction was made between ordinary word processor documents and more complicated page layouts. When you start Pages 08 or 09, though, you are presented with the Template Chooser which separates word processing templates from page layout templates.

There's a good reason for this. When you create an ordinary word processor document, you want it to keep adding pages automatically as you type. When you work on page layouts, though, you start with a fixed number of pages in mind and adjust the length or size of your text to suit. Other word processing programs (like Word, for example), don't offer this distinction and this can cause confusion where documents have to fit specific page lengths and with pages designed in a certain way.

Back to our letter...

1 You can start with a Blank template and create the letter from scratch, or choose one of the other letter templates. The Typewriter template looks good, so we'll use that.

2 You may find that the sheet in the typewriter image contains your name and contact details. Pages gets this from the user

information you entered when you first set up your new Mac. To change any of this information, just double-click this object. You can now select any of the text by dragging the cursor over it, and type in new text instead.

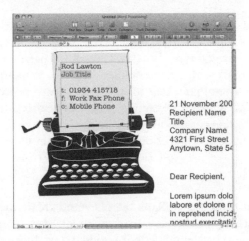

3 Now you'll want to type in the name and address of the recipient. You'll find that simply clicking on a line selects the whole line. That's because this is placeholder text specifically designed for typing over, and it's widely used in Pages templates.

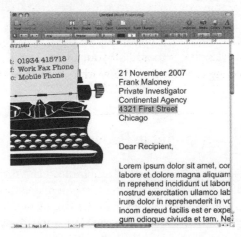

4 The main body of the letter is in what looks like Latin, but this is just dummy text. Again, clicking it once selects all this dummy text and you can simply type in the content of your own letter.

And that's it, you've used Pages to write a letter. You can now experiment with different fonts, sizes and styles for the text using the menus at the top of the window.

Author insight

The templates in Pages are a great way to get started because they don't drop you in at the deep end. You can see how your finished document might look straight away, and even though you've still got to add all your own content, you still have the feeling that most of the work's already been done.

6.3 Designing a leaflet in Pages

Now let's try something a little more ambitious. Let's say you want to design a leaflet for your new business. If you take a look at the Brochures in the Page Layout section of the Template Chooser, you'll see there are quite a few to choose from. How about Classic Brochure?

1 The template opens up as a document that looks almost ready to print. All you have to do is type in your own text over the placeholder text that's in the template.

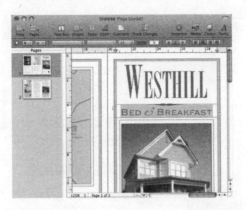

2 There may be other things you need to change, too, e.g. the photos in the template with some of your own. To do this, click the **Media** button at the top of the Pages window.

3 The Media palette has three sections, for **Audio, Photos** and **Music**. It's the Photos section that's relevant here, and if you select this you'll see that it displays the contents of your iPhoto library. How clever is that? It's typical of the way Apple seamlessly integrates all these different Mac applications.

4 When you've found the photo you want in your library, drag it off the palette and onto the placeholder that you want to replace. Your new photo will be automatically sized to fit.

5 If you want to change the colours, click the **Inspector** button to display the Inspector palette. To change the colour of an object, click the palette's **Graphic** button, then click on the object. Its Fill colour will be displayed directly below, and to change the colour simply click on it and choose a new one from the Colors palette. To change the colour of text, double-click the box the text is in – this selects all the text. You can now click the Inspector's **Text** button to change the text colour.

In practice, some of the Pages templates are quite complex, with some objects layered on top of others, and it can take a little while to work out which items you need to edit and how, but the tools themselves are quite straightforward.

The most interesting feature, though, is to be found in the vertical Pages display at the far left of the screen. You'll see that templates often have two or more pages, and that these pages have different but themed layouts. You can add more pages at will, and you do this using the Pages button, top left.

And here's the next surprise – you can add ready-designed pages to those already in a document, and you have a choice of several layouts, depending on the template. You don't have to struggle to fill blank pages because they're already filled – all you have to do is type in your own text and add your own photos!

The main differences with Pages 09 are an increased choice of templates, a new outlining system for organizing your thoughts, the ability to carry out mail merge with information from a Numbers spreadsheet and compatibility with MathType and EndNote, which are separately-available tools used by academics and engineers to incorporate mathematical formulae and bibliographic references.

Author insight

Pages is so good at laying out documents with text, pictures, charts and tables, that you really don't need a traditional DTP style program at all for this kind of work, and that makes the iWork suite even more of a bargain.

6.4 Creating a Keynote presentation

Word processing is one of the most common computing tasks of all, whether you're working in an office or writing a letter at home. But quite often we also need to produce presentations, and not just for work colleagues and customers – schools often ask students to submit homework and coursework as a presentation, too.

Presentations are effectively slideshows run from a computer and projected on to a screen in front of an audience. Usually, the author stands at the front talking through the main points, though this is not essential.

Microsoft Office users will be familiar with PowerPoint, its presentations tool. Apple's equivalent in iWork is Keynote. If you've used PowerPoint, then you won't find it difficult to get to grips with Keynote. The principle is the same – the presentation is made up of a series of slides onto which you can place text and pictures. One slide can be made to fade into the next using transitions, and it's possible to make objects appear on the slides one by one as you explain your ideas to the audience.

Keynote, like Pages, comes with a collection of templates to make it easier to get started. These are themed presentation designs, and it has to be said that they are much more elegant and modern-looking than those you get in Microsoft PowerPoint.

1   Once you've chosen the design, for example Blueprint, the first slide is created. In the case of the Blueprint theme, this is a title page with two text boxes which both say **Double-click to edit**. Do just that to enter your own title and strap line.

2 Now you're ready to start adding slides. To do this, click the '+' button in the top left-hand corner of the Keynote window. This creates a new slide with a different layout that's still part of the overall design theme. If you don't like the layout or it's not suitable for the information you want to convey, click the Masters button at the top of the window and choose a new design.

3 To change the text, double-click a text box. To change a picture, open the Media palette and drag across a new one from your iPhoto library.

Author insight

Most of us dread going to presentations almost as much as we dread having to create them. But they don't need to be dull. Keynote gets you off to a good start with some great-looking design themes, but the real secret is rehearsal. It's only when you practise making the presentation (an empty room is fine!) that you realize where the dead spots and awkward explanations might be.

If you're unfamiliar with presentations, the best way to understand what Keynote can do is simply to experiment with slides and layouts and your own content, then play back the presentation to see what it looks like. To do this, select the first slide (they're displayed in the vertical Slides panel on the left) and click the Play button above.

You can enhance your presentations considerably by animating the objects on your slide and adding transitions between slides. That's a little outside the scope of this book, but it's not too difficult to pick up the basics from the online Help and from the tutorials on the Apple website.

This is one area where Keynote 09 has some big advantages over Keynote 08. A new Magic Move feature makes it easy to move an object to a new position on the next slide, there are some new and very sophisticated text and object transitions and you can even animate 3D charts.

Author insight

If you've used PowerPoint's sound effects and you're wondering where Keynote's are, you can stop looking. There aren't any. You can add a music soundtrack, or movies with sound, but that's it. It's a limitation in some ways, but probably a good thing in others because unless you're a professional multimedia designer, simplicity is usually best.

6.5 Adding a chart

You can add more to Keynote slides than just words and pictures. You'll see that there are buttons at the top of the window for adding Shapes, Tables and Charts. These options are also available in Pages, by the way, and also in Numbers, which we'll come to shortly.

Explaining all of Keynote's features in depth would take up a whole book, whereas we only have a chapter in which to cover all three iWork programs. What we can do, though, is demonstrate just one of these features – charts.

Charts (or graphs) are a great way to present data in a more convincing or a more understandable fashion. Let's take a simple example. Imagine you're the treasurer of a club and that you need to illustrate how much is spent on premises, equipment and advertising as a proportion of the club's total outgoings.

1 Pie charts are ideal for illustrating this kind of data, so the first step is to create a new, blank slide and then click the **Charts** button to display a pop-up list of chart types – pie charts are near the bottom.

2 Keynote now creates a pie chart on the slide, together with a **Chart Data Editor** window which contains the data used to create the chart. Now at the moment, this contains dummy data you need to replace.

3 Double-click the cells in the **Data Editor** and type in your own data. Don't forget to change the row and column headings at the same time.

4 If there are extra columns of dummy data that you don't need, just click the column heading to select the whole column and press [**Backspace**] to delete it. To add columns or rows, just type directly into blank cells. When you make changes in the **Data Editor** window, the chart itself updates automatically.

6.6 Introducing spreadsheets

Finally, we'll take a look at Numbers, the brand new spreadsheet application introduced in iWork 08. This is equivalent to the Excel spreadsheet program in Microsoft Office, though Numbers works slightly differently from Excel, so that even if you are already familiar with spreadsheet programs, you're going to find Numbers a little different, to say the least.

First things first, though. If you don't know anything about spreadsheets, they can seem extremely complex and daunting things. In principle, though, they are quite simple.

We all know how to work a pocket calculator. You enter a calculation, press the [=] key and the answer appears in the display. The trouble with calculators, though, is that they can only do one calculation at a time, and they forget the last one as soon as you begin the next.

A single spreadsheet is like a vast army of pocket calculators, all of which remember your calculations indefinitely.

Think of each spreadsheet cell as a single calculator's display. You type the calculation into that cell, which then displays the answer. The difference is, though, that these calculations can be based on the contents of other cells, and each cell has a unique reference (or 'address') to make this possible.

That's why spreadsheets use letters to identify columns and numbers for rows. Using a combination of column letter and cell number, you can identify each unique cell. This is called a cell reference, and it takes the form A6, or G7 and so on.

A simple example will make this clearer.

1 Open a new Numbers document. You'll be presented with an empty spreadsheet.

2 Click on cell B2 and type in the number '2'. Click on cell B3 below it and type '2'. Now click on cell B4 below and type '=' and then click on cell B2. Now type a 'plus' sign ('+') and click on cell B3.

3 As you do this, you'll see that Numbers is recording your calculation in a black Formula box (formula is the spreadsheet term for a calculation). It should now read '=B2+B3'. If so, press the green tick button to the right.

	A	B	C
1			
2		2	
3		2	
4	=B2+B3		
5			
6			
7			

4 Cell B4 now contains the result of adding cell B2 to cell B3. (We can now breathe a sigh of relief that 2 plus 2 does indeed equal 4.)

	A	B	C
1			
2		2	
3		2	
4		4	
5			
6			
7			

5 But now that we've set it up, this formula will continue to work even if we change the contents of cells B2 and B3. We can type in '16' and '23', for example, and it'll add these up too.

	A	B	C
1			
2		16	
3		23	
4		39	
5			
6			
7			

This is just scratching the surface, of course. Spreadsheets are capable of carrying out fiendishly complicated calculations in the blink of an eye, but this simple example should at least make it easier to understand how they do it.

6.7 What's different about Numbers

If you're used to conventional spreadsheet programs like Microsoft Excel, Numbers is going to look both familiar and strange at the same time. The spreadsheets themselves look much the same, but instead of extending off the screen as a practically infinite array of rows and columns, in Numbers they are a finite size. What you see on the screen is not the whole spreadsheet, but what Numbers calls a 'table'.

In fact, you can create many 'tables' on the same sheet, and they can be as big or as small as you like. This enables you to visually separate blocks of data, and this in turn makes it easier to understand and control how this data interacts.

Let's take a simple example. You want to prepare a list of your business's outgoings, and another listing sources of income. Then we can subtract one from the other to calculate the profit.

1 First, select the default table created in new documents by clicking its top left-hand corner and then press [**Backspace**] to delete it. This leaves you with a completely blank page.

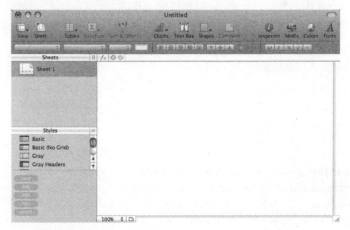

2 Now click the **Tables** button at the top of the window. This displays a list of table styles. We want the Headers table style.

3 The new table has four columns for data where we only need one. To delete columns, move the mouse pointer over the right-hand side to display an arrow. Click this to open a drop-down menu and click the **Delete Column** option.

4 This leaves us with a table consisting of a single column with a title row and the top and row headings on the left. We can now type in our headings and data.

5 When that's done, we need to total up the individual outgoings. Select the empty cell directly below the column of figures, click the **Function** button at the top of the window and choose **Sum** from the menu. This cell will now display the total. If there are any blank rows left below, these can be deleted using the pop-up menus at the left-hand end of the rows.

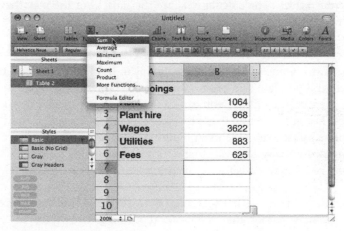

6 This process can be repeated for the company's sources of income. Finally, we can create a third, smaller table with just a heading ('Profit') and a single cell. To calculate the profit, we select this cell, type '=' and then click on the total income cell in the Income table. Next, we type '-' and then click on the total cell in the Outgoings table to complete the formula.

This hasn't achieved anything that couldn't have been done in Excel, but the data is now clearly separated and distinguished in different tables. The calculations are the same, but the way they're carried out is much easier to grasp visually.

This is not the only noteworthy characteristic of Numbers by any means. Charts too can be created as individual objects on the sheet, and you can add photos and other graphics to Numbers documents as readily as you can to Pages documents and Keynote slides. It's possible to create very sophisticated, compelling and graphically rich documents in Numbers and it's a much more sophisticated way of presenting data to clients and colleagues than a regular spreadsheet application like Excel can manage.

The main differences between Numbers 08 and Numbers 09 are that the new version makes it easier to add and keep track of functions. These are more advanced calculations for things like compound interest rates and scientific conversions. And a new feature called 'categories' means you can subdivide lists of data into groups, and this makes it easier to create subtotals. For example, you could group and subtotal all your transactions by month.

Author insight

The separate tables in Numbers are clever enough, but the ability to add headers and footers makes them better still. You no longer have to work out how to separate column headers from the data itself, or how to keep subtotals at the bottom when you add more rows.

6.8 Swapping documents with others

Of course, not everyone you work with will be using iWork. You may frequently find yourself swapping files with Microsoft Office users (PC or Mac), so you may be faced with the problem of opening Office files that others send you or finding ways to send them files created in iWork that they can open using their Microsoft Office applications.

The best way to do this is to find a file format that both sets of programs can work with. iWork can open Office files directly, whether they were created in Word, Excel or PowerPoint, or on the PC or the Mac.

Transferring files the other way, from iWork to Office, may not be so straightforward. The problem is that the iWork applications offer some features which simply don't exist in their Office counterparts, and this is especially true of Numbers.

The iWork applications can, however, export documents in Office formats and attempt to preserve the document formatting and features as far as possible in the process.

Ultimately, though, if a large part of your work does involve swapping files with Office users, you might be better off using Office yourself. Paradoxically, this is not because iWork is inferior. In fact, it's because there are things you can do in iWork which simply don't have counterparts in Office.

TEST

1 *Pages can create documents in two different modes according to your needs. What are they?*

2 *How do you get pictures from your iPhoto library into your documents?*

3 *What is a 'placeholder'.*

4 *What is the basic building block of a presentation?*

5 *What's the difference between transitions and animations?*

6 *You can choose a design 'theme' for your presentation, but within this you can also choose different layouts for each slide. What are these called and where do you find them?*

7 *In Microsoft Excel, a 'spreadsheet' extends off the screen with a large number of rows and columns. What's different about Numbers?*

8 *How would you add up a column of figures in Numbers?*

9 *What's the correct term for the calculations you type into spreadsheet cells?*

10 *How do you work with Microsoft Office files in iWork?*

Mac Office 2008

In this chapter you will learn:
* *why Office makes sense for Mac users*
* *how the Mac and Windows versions of Office compare*
* *how to get started with Word*
* *about outlines in Word*
* *how to add graphics to documents*
* *about Excel's List Manager*
* *how to create a PowerPoint presentation*
* *what Entourage can do*

7.1 No Mac is an island!

There was a time when using a Mac meant that you risked cutting yourself off from the regular world of PCs, and swapping files or any kind of data could be a difficult, technical process. That was long ago. Today, Macs and PCs co-exist perfectly happily, and this is explained in much more detail in Chapter 8.

Microsoft Word   Microsoft Excel

Microsoft PowerPoint   Microsoft Entourage

This co-existence is easier still if the PC and Mac users are using the same software, because files can then be opened, viewed and edited on both machines without any kind of conversion.

Your PC-using colleague can send you an Excel worksheet to amend, you can modify it on your Mac, send it back and they can open it again just as if it had been worked on using a PC.

That's the big advantage of using Microsoft Office on a Mac for those in a business environment populated largely by Windows PCs (and such environments tend to use Microsoft Office applications almost exclusively).

We cover Office 2008 in this chapter because it's the latest version, though (at the time of writing) Office 2011 is expected in late 2010. Most of the techniques and explanations apply to earlier versions too, though, and only the interface and tools have changed.

Office on the Mac is almost identical to the PC version, with Word, Excel and PowerPoint, but it has its own personal information manager, Entourage.

7.2 Mac Office vs Windows Office

The Mac and Windows versions share the same core applications: Word, Excel and PowerPoint, but there are differences in the secondary applications.

The main difference is that the Windows version of office comes with an email/personal organizer application called Outlook, which doesn't have a Mac version. Instead, Mac users get a program called Entourage. This does the same job, managing your mail, your contacts, appointments and tasks, but looks and works very differently.

This looks set to change with the release of Office 2011, though, which will include a new Mac version of Outlook. Microsoft says it won't be exactly the same as the Windows version, but there will be a high level of compatibility. It should also be more efficient than Entourage, too.

The Windows version of Office comes in several editions, too, and the higher-level editions include programs not available on the Mac, notably the Access relational database application (designed for database programmers rather than everyday users) and the Publisher desktop publishing application (Pages can do this job very well on the Mac).

There are minor differences too between the Mac and PC versions of Word, PowerPoint and Excel, but these are mostly down to the look and feel of the interface. The Mac versions use a floating Formatting Palette while the PC versions rely on toolbars or ribbons, depending on the version (Office 2003 or 2007).

For those who mainly use Word, Excel and PowerPoint, there's really not much to choose between the Mac and PC versions at all, and Mac Office 2008 is in no way the poor relation to Windows Office 2003 or 2007.

7.3 Mac Office vs iWork

By now, you will be aware that the three core applications in Mac Office – word processor, spreadsheet and presentations tool – are matched by the same three program types in Apple's iWork. So should you use Office, or should you use iWork?

iWork is much cheaper, different, but equally powerful in its own way and, it has to be said, it looks and behaves like it belongs to a new generation of software, whereas Office 2008, despite a cosmetic overhaul, is definitely 'old school'. For domestic users who don't have to swap files with Windows machines on a regular basis, iWork is more attractive and simpler. But for those who work alongside PCs all day, whether on the same site or via email, Office 2008 is the most practical solution because there are no difficulties over inconsistencies in the way documents are formatted. This becomes particularly important if you have to collaborate with others over documents, financial worksheets or presentations.

Author insight

Office or iWork? If you're working on your own, iWork is simpler, easier and more up-to-date, with fewer pitfalls for the unwary. But even though you can export Office-compatible versions of your files if necessary to send to co-workers, it just adds another layer of complication you don't need. For business use, then, Office is likely to be the better choice.

7.4 Microsoft Word basics

When you launch Microsoft Word, it doesn't create a new, blank document straight away. Instead, it launches into the Project Gallery, where Office 2008's collection of templates for Word, Excel and PowerPoint are combined into a single window. You may find this useful if you regularly use the templates supplied with the program, but you may find it annoying if you prefer to start from scratch or from existing documents (it also appears when you start Excel or PowerPoint).

When you start Word, Excel or PowerPoint, you can choose a ready-made document template from the Project Gallery.

To disable it, click the Gallery's last section, **Customize**, and de-select the box labelled **Show Project Gallery at startup.**

To create a new, blank Word document, either select this option in the Project Gallery's **New** section or, if you have disabled the Project Gallery as we've just described, Word will simply start up with a new, blank document.

Try it out – just start typing. To change the font, text size or style, just select the text by dragging the cursor over it and choose the options you want to change from the floating Formatting Palette.

If it's not visible, use the **View > Formatting Palette** menu command. This palette is arranged vertically in a series of sections, each of which can be expanded by clicking the arrow to the left of its title and collapsed by clicking the arrow again.

You can use the Formatting Palette to add objects like tables and graphics, format text and apply predefined text styles. These styles include a series of headings, labelled 'Heading 1', 'Heading 2' and so on. These have a special significance in Word, as we'll see in the next section.

7.5 Outlining in Word

For everyday use, Word can seem a little complicated and overpowering compared with Pages, but it has advantages for business users (it's easy to swap files with PCs) and for technical and academic authors (outside the scope of this book). It's also rather good at a technique called Outlining which is a way of getting down your ideas and developing them into finished text. (It's also possible to do this in Pages 09, by the way.)

Word has a special Outline mode. You can enter it by choosing Outline from the View menu. Once you're in this mode you're able to organize, develop and structure your ideas in a way that's simply not possible with conventional, 'linear' writing. Here's a quick introduction to how it works:

1 Start off by typing an idea or a topic. By default, this will appear in Word's 'Normal' style, which is ideal for what follows. Now switch

to the Outline mode using the **View** menu. You'll note that each paragraph now has a square symbol to its left. This is used for dragging paragraphs from one place to another or for selecting the whole paragraph with a single click. The significance of this will become apparent shortly.

2 Imagine you're writing an essay. The subject doesn't matter – it can be anything you like. Don't even try to organize it into a logical order in your head before you start typing. Instead, type in every idea on a single line, as it occurs to you. Keep going until you've written down everything you can think of for the time being. You should now have a long list of ideas. This is the raw material; the starting point. It's

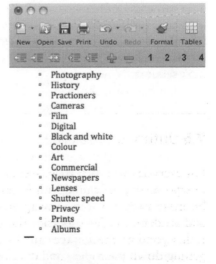

similar to a technique called freewriting, which is used by some authors. It's much more important to first get everything down – you can sort it out into some kind of order later. And that's the next step in the Outlining process.

3 Go back over your list. You'll notice two things. The first is that many of the ideas are in the wrong order. This is easy to put right. To move an item, simply drag its square symbol up or down, reorganizing your ideas into something like their correct order.

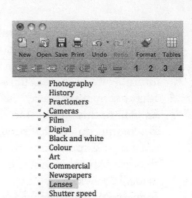

4 But you'll also notice something else. Not all of your ideas will be of equal significance. Some will be sub-topics of others – and this is where you can start organizing them into a hierarchy of headings and subheadings. Start by picking a main topic – click on the square symbol to its left to select it. Now use the [**Shift**]-[**Tab**] shortcut. This promotes the topic to a heading.

5 Find any subheadings for this topic. Make sure they're moved up so that they're beneath the heading, select one of these topics and hit [**Tab**]. This demotes the topic to a subheading. (To start with, all the topics are in the body text style. This is the lowest of the low in the heading hierarchy.)

6 Now you can go through all the topics, moving them, promoting them and demoting them until they're organized into a hierarchical structure.

7 As you do this, you'll start to see other topics that need adding, and spot connections to other areas that you should include and explore. The outlining process encourages your mind to think 'outwards', where conventional writing tends to focus it 'inwards' along very linear paths. When you're satisfied that your outline is complete, your document will consist of a complete set of headings and subheadings.

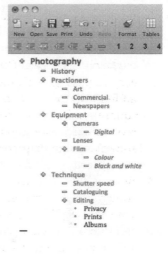

8 With this structure in place, writing the main body text is suddenly so much easier because now you know what you've got to write! To use the body text style, use the **[Shift]**-**[Command]**-**[N]** shortcut, or choose **Normal** from the text style menu on the toolbar. This outlining system completely banishes the dreaded 'blank page' syndrome that can stop even experienced writers dead in their tracks.

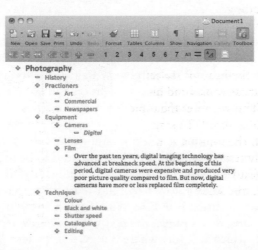

When you've filled in the body text, you can revert to Normal or Page Layout view using the **View** menu. Page Layout view is best if you want to see exactly how your pages will print as you work, and especially if you want to insert graphics or photos.

> **Author insight**
>
> Outlining is a terrific way of writing because it enables you to plan what you're going to say before you start writing. But even though Pages 09 now has a very good outlining mode, Word is still the best.

7.6 Inserting graphics in Word

It's easy to add graphics to a Word document either by dragging them from a Finder window on to the document window, or by opening the Insert menu and choosing the Picture command.

If you drag graphics on to the document, you'll see the insertion point moving around the text as you drag the mouse pointer. This indicates where the graphic will be inserted when you release the mouse button. If you use the menu command instead, first place the insertion point where you want the graphic to go.

By default, Word inserts graphics as inline objects. That means they are embedded in the text, so that if the text moves because of editing changes, the graphic moves with it. This can be useful, but sometimes you want the graphic to stay where you put it and for the text to flow around it, as it might on a magazine page. To do this, change the graphic's text wrap properties.

1 Click on the graphic to select it, and expand the **Wrapping** section in the **Formatting** palette (you need to be in Normal or Page Layout view to do this, not Outline view).
2 Click on the **Style** button to display a list of wrap options. The current setting is **In Line With Text**, but if you change it to **Square**, for example, the text will now flow around the graphic, which will stay where it is even if the text moves.

Actually, that's not quite true. The graphic is still anchored to the text to the extent that it will move to another page if the text it's anchored to does. This is Microsoft's attempt to make Word foolproof, but in fact it makes it terribly confusing for those attempting to use Word like a desktop publishing program, when its behaviour can seem utterly unpredictable.

The alternative, for those using Word 2008, is to use the new Publishing Layout mode. Word 2008 is like Pages, in that it offers both a conventional word processor environment and a page layout mode. In Word 2008, you can switch your document between the two modes, whereas in Pages you can't. However, Word's page layout tools aren't quite as predictable or as straightforward.

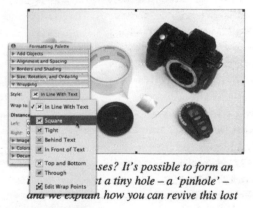

It's easy to insert pictures in Word documents, but you do need to understand how the text wrapping options work.

Author insight

You can use Word to produce brochures, fliers and other elaborate layouts, but it makes a bit of a meal of it and it's not really in its element. Where it really scores is a straightforward word-processor, and it's particularly good for academics, technical authors, thanks to its ability to generate tables of contents, indices, cross-references and bibliographies.

7.7 Excel basics

Microsoft Excel has long been considered the standard professional spreadsheet application amongst statisticians, engineers, accountants and many other technical professionals.

We have explained in Chapter 6 how spreadsheets work. What we will do here is highlight an area in Excel which is often overlooked – its ability to create and manage lists.

List is another word for database. You could, for example, prepare a list of invoices to customers. Here's how it's done:

1 First, use the **Insert > List menu** command. This runs the List wizard, which walks you through the process in three steps. First, you're asked where your list data is (this only applies if you already have data which you want to convert into a list) and where you want the list to be created – select **New worksheet**.

2 Now click the **Next** button to go to step 2. Here you're asked to choose the column headings for your list. In our example, we want the first column to have the heading 'Job', so we type 'Job' into the **Column name** box and click the **Add** button.

3 We need to add a column for the customer name, so now we type 'Customer' into the box and click the **Add** button again.

4 Next, we need a column heading for 'Amount', but here the procedure is slightly different. Before clicking **Add**, open the **Data type** pop-up menu directly below the box and choose **Currency** from the list.

5 Add a fourth column heading, 'Date due', and this time choose **Date** from the **Data type** menu.

6 Click the **Next** button. We're now on step 3, where we can choose a name for the list (if required) and check the Show totals row box. Now click Finish.

The finished list doesn't look like a regular worksheet. The usual spreadsheet grid is gone, and the list is isolated in its own white space. The headings are separated from the first row, which is empty. Start by typing in the first invoice. As you do, you'll notice that Excel creates a new, blank line directly below. This is ready for you to type in the next invoice, and so on. You'll also see a 'Total row' appear at the bottom.

Type in some more invoices. By default, the Total row totals up the last column. This is the due date for our invoices, so the total is meaningless. To fix this, click the pop-up in the right-hand corner of that Total cell and choose (No formula) from the list. Now, click the pop-up in the Total cell under the 'Amount' column, and choose Sum from the list. Now, this cell will display the total value of all our invoices. This assumes special significance when we look at the AutoFilters for each column...

The column headings each have a pop-up menu alongside them, too. These are the AutoFilters. You can use these menus to do two things: (a) to sort your invoices by Job, Customer and so on, depending on which column heading you're working with, and (b) to 'filter' the data according to a specific Job, Customer and so on. These menus list each unique name or value in that column, so identifying and selecting them is easy.

When you AutoFilter a column in this way, two things happen. The first is that the list now only shows those matching items. Second, the Total row now adds up only the items currently being shown. For example, you could do this to isolate all the jobs you've done for a particular customer and get a total amount owed by that customer for those jobs.

Excel's Lists offer a very quick and useful way of compiling and analysing information. And they remain quick (and become even more useful!) when you have hundreds or even thousands of records to sort through.

Job	Customer	Amount	Date	(New Column)
Plastering	Jones	£224.00	12/18	
Papering	Smith	£198.00	12/10	
Sanding	Brown	£88.00	12/8	
Rendering	Brown	£144.00	12/8	
Total		**£654.00**		

List Wizard   Column Settings

List ▾   Autofilters   Total Row   Visuals

Author insight

In some ways, Excel now looks rather primitive compared to Numbers, but in one respect at least it's still the best. You can use it to create Lists (databases, effectively) with AutoFilters which provide incredibly fast searches and summaries.

7.8 PowerPoint basics

PowerPoint is Microsoft Office's presentations tool. Many computer users might go through their whole career without ever needing to create a presentation, or even knowing what one is, but increasingly they're becoming part of the armoury of any keen executive. They're also becoming popular in schools as students are encouraged more and more to use PowerPoint to develop their essays, coursework and class presentations.

PowerPoint can look complicated, but presentations are actually quite simple. Once you understand the principles they're based on, everything falls into place. In addition, PowerPoint is really very similar to Apple's Keynote, described in Chapter 6. Once you understand one, you understand the other.

Every presentation is basically a slideshow. And each slide is a single screen of information. This information could be a title, a heading, a series of bullet points, a chart, a photo or a diagram – or combinations of all of those.

When you make your presentation you show each slide in turn, pausing as necessary to explain certain points in more depth. PowerPoint has a feature called 'speaker notes' which lets you type in notes and information for your own reference when making presentations – these speaker notes are not visible to the audience.

To make your presentations look more professional, you can add transitions to make one slide fade into the next, and you can animate objects on the slide so that bullet points appear one by one, for example.

Using PowerPoint can be as simple or as complicated as you want to make it. It's best to start with something simple, like one of the preset templates, and experiment with the more advanced options as you go along.

PowerPoint 2004 did come with a wider selection of templates than PowerPoint 2008, many of which came with pre-designed slides and content which gave you some clues about what to say and when to say it. The choice in PowerPoint 2008 is smaller, but you can browse through a wide variety of templates on the Microsoft Office Online site at office.microsoft.com/en-us/templates. Most of these are designed for Office 2003 or Office 2007 on the PC, but Office 2008 on the Mac can open them directly.

1 This is a ready-made presentation called 'Making Public Speaking Easier' which has been downloaded from the Office site. It's displayed here in Normal view, with thumbnail versions of the slides displayed in a vertical list on the left. You can click on any thumbnail to view that slide in the main window.

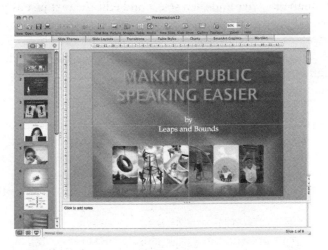

2 But you can also display the list of slides as an outline, just like those you can create in Microsoft Word. You can toggle between the thumbnail and outline views using the buttons at the top of this sidebar. In Outline mode, each heading corresponds to a slide title, and if you create subheadings under a title, these appear as bullet points on the slide.

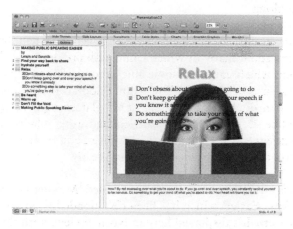

3 Slides typically consists of a mixture of text boxes and graphics. Some templates have 'placeholder' text you can simply click on to type over. Otherwise, click on a text box to make it active and then select and edit the text just as you would in a word processor. In PowerPoint, different text boxes have different roles. This is the slide 'Title' box.

4 You can add pictures simply by dragging them on to a slide from a **Finder** window. You move them into position by dragging them from the centre, and you can resize them by dragging on the corner handles. When you start designing your own slides, you'll need to display the Drawing toolbar, seen here on the right. To do this, you use the **View > Toolbars** menu.

5 Office 2008 has a new Gallery feature, which is displayed when you click on the **Gallery** button on the toolbar. You can use this to insert new slides, using the **Slide Layouts** tab to browse the preset designs available. These can also be applied to existing slides.

6 Finally, if you decide you don't like the fonts and colour scheme used in your presentation, you can change these too by choosing a different Slide Theme from the Gallery. These can be applied to individual slides, or all the slides in your presentation.

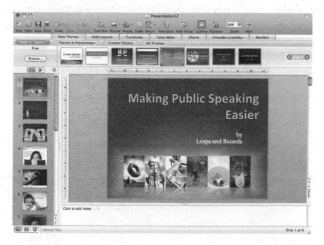

Obviously there's a lot more to PowerPoint than this, but the key to getting up and running quickly with this program, as with so many others, is to start with something simple that makes sense straight away, and then build on that as and when you're ready to take on more complicated ideas.

7.9 Entourage – unique to the Mac

While the Mac's versions of Word, Excel and PowerPoint are quite similar to the Windows version, there's no Mac version of Outlook, the email and personal information manager on the PC. Instead, Microsoft developed a wholly new application called Entourage, which does the same jobs, but looks very different from Outlook. Entourage is a single program, but with six distinct sections: Mail, Address Book, Calendar, Notes, Tasks and Project Centre. These are accessed by buttons clustered in the top left-hand corner of the Entourage window.

If you click the Mail button, you'll see a list of mail folders on the left, and a list of messages in the current folder on the right – though the layout can be customized, so yours may be different. For example, you can use the **View > Preview Pane** command to display a preview pane either below the messages or to its right. When you click on a message title, its contents are displayed in this pane. Entourage's online Help explains the display and other options available, so we won't go into detail here. (The basics of email are explained in Chapter 5.)

The one other thing you will need to know is how to set up your email accounts in Entourage.

1 Use the **Tools > Accounts** command to open the **Accounts** window.
2 Click the **New** button to create an account. The Account Setup Assistant then walks you through the process in easy steps – you will need the email account information from your service provider or email host.

But why would you want to use Entourage for email when you already have the Mail program supplied with the Mac? It's largely a matter of preference. Your author prefers Mail, but others may prefer Entourage – it is sometimes useful to be able to link emails with appointments and appointments with files. This integration of your office tasks is what Entourage is designed for.

The Address Book is where Entourage stores email addresses, phone numbers and street addresses. Your lists of contacts can be sorted alphabetically by name or company, for example, by clicking the column headings at the top of the lists. Again, the Mac already has an Address Book of its own, so whether or not you'll find the Entourage Address Book useful will depend on how you like to work and how useful you find Entourage to be.

It's the same situation with the Calendar. Here, you can plan holidays, enter appointments and set up meetings – when you set up a meeting, you can also invite people in your Address Book by email with just a few button clicks. You may find this kind of integration of your office tasks indispensable, but be aware that it can also force you into an unnecessarily complex and regimented way of working – it's a double-edged sword. The Calendar in Entourage is an alternative to Apple's own iCal. Again, the decision you face is whether to use the Apple software that comes with the Mac for these jobs, or whether to move all your data across into Entourage. They don't share the same data, so it's going to have to be one or the other.

The Notes section is a place where you can jot down ideas or information that don't justify an entire document on their own, while the Tasks section is where you list all the jobs you've got to do, the date they have to be done by and their priority. The Apple alternative to this is the To Do list in iCal and Mail.

It's clear, then, that Entourage is a very sophisticated personal organizer application that can do a great job of keeping your work life running smoothly. It's also clear, though, that you can do pretty well all of these things using the free Apple software pre-installed on the Mac.

Entourage has six sections, accessed by the buttons top left: Mail, Address Book, Calendar, Notes, Tasks, Project Center. This is Entourage 2004, but Entourage 2008 has only minor interface differences.

So which do you use? On the one hand, Entourage integrates all these jobs very well and also dovetails very well with the other Office applications and centralized company networks. However, other programs apart from Office are more likely to integrate with the Apple software. You may also find the Apple alternatives rather simpler to understand and more direct in their approach.

Author insight

Entourage is a bit of an uneasy addition to the Mac Office suite because of the way it crosses over with iCal, Apple Mail and the Mac's Address Book. It's due to be replaced by Outlook in Office 2011, but there's still going to be the same duplication.

7.10 Managing your projects

But for managers with a very organized approach to their work, Entourage has the advantage. And this is reflected in its sixth section, the Project Center. Here's how it works (again, these screenshots are from Entourage 2004, but the differences in 2008 are superficial):

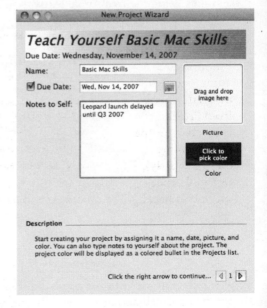

1 Click the **New Project** button and type in a title. Let's call it 'Teach Yourself Basic Mac Skills'. We also need to set a deadline and, if we have a suitable image, we can drag it into the box on the right as a visual reminder. Underneath, you can jot down any relevant notes about the project, if applicable.

2 In the next step, you can create or set up Project Watch folders. Any documents or other items added to these folders subsequently will automatically appear in that project in Entourage.

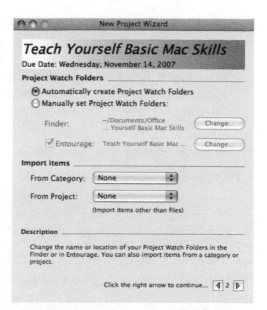

3 In the next step you can instruct Entourage to automatically associate emails from Project contacts with the project (more on this shortly), or emails about specific subjects.

4 The fourth step is a summary of your settings, and when you OK this step, you're returned to the Project Center where you can view your new project. This has a number of different tabs, but the first is the Overview. This displays a calendar at the top, a task window below and, at the bottom a list of related email messages and documents. As time goes by, these lists will be populated automatically.

5 Finally, you will need to associate relevant contacts with the project, and you do this using the **Contacts** tab and clicking the **Add** button to select them from your Address Book.

There's a lot more to Entourage's Project Center than we have the space to cover here, but this simple walkthrough should have made it easier to see what it sets out to do and how it works. It's when you undertake complex management tasks like these that Entourage begins to pull its weight, but we repeat our earlier warning that Entourage can lure you into setting up procedures which appear efficient but are actually rather more complex and bureaucratic than they need to be.

Besides, Entourage won't be with us for much longer...

Office 2011 is coming

Microsoft is planning to launch Office 2008's successor, Office 2011, late in 2010. One of the most significant changes will be the replacement of Entourage with a Mac version of Outlook, the personal information manager that comes with Office on the PC. It's expected to be cleaner, simpler and faster than Entourage, and compatible with the Windows version.

There's no indication of major changes within Word, Excel and PowerPoint in terms of features, but their interface will be updated to make it more 'Mac-like'.

Instead, Microsoft is devoting much of its attention to enhancing the 'workflow' and 'collaboration' tools. Office is designed not just for single users, after all, and is often used in larger workgroups in projects with several authors and contributors.

TEST

1 Where can you find Office's collection of pre-designed document templates?

2 What special feature in Word helps you organize your ideas before you start writing?

3 You can add photos and other graphics to Word documents as one of two different types of object. What are they, and what's the difference?

4 If you want to design more sophisticated layouts in Word, such as leaflets or newsletters, what's the best way to do it?

5 Microsoft Excel can carry out calculations like any other spreadsheet, but what special feature allows it to work like a database?

6 What's an AutoFilter?

7 You can display your PowerPoint presentation as a series of slides in the sidebar on the left, but what's the other option, and why is it useful?

8 What are 'speaker notes'?

9 What's the difference between Slide Layouts and Slide Themes.

10 Microsoft is dropping the Entourage personal information manager in Office 2011, but what is it being replaced with?

8

Working with PCs

In this chapter you will learn:
- *how to transfer files by email*
- *ways to transfer larger files via the Internet*
- *the relative usefulness of CDs, DVDs, hard disks and stick drives*
- *how to connect to a PC network*
- *how to make sure files are compatible*

8.1 Swapping files

You may be delighted with your new Mac, but you still have
to get on with other computer users. The vast majority of
computers out there are PCs, and you're going to have to find
a way to work alongside them. We're not talking about those
arguments in the pub about which computer is best, but purely
practical considerations, like transferring your child's homework
assignment to the PCs at school, or working on your boss's
report when he or she uses a PC at the office and you're using
your Mac at home.

There are two issues here. One is finding a way to get files from the
Mac to the PC and vice versa. The other is making sure that the PC
can read the Mac's files, and that the Mac can read the PC's.

Windows PCs make little attempt to acknowledge the existence
of Macs or work with them. Fortunately, Apple, recognizing

the Mac's minority status perhaps, have gone to great lengths to accommodate Windows PCs.

We'll look at ways of making sure both machines can work with the same files, but first we'll look at how to get these files from one computer to the other. A few years ago this might have been a bit of a stumbling block, but now it's easy.

SEND FILES BY EMAIL OR THE INTERNET

Just about everyone, whether they own a PC or a Mac, uses email. And as long as the files aren't too large (anything under 5Mb should be fine) you can simply attach the file to the email. It's as simple as that. You have to make sure the file is one that the PC can read, of course, and we'll look at that a little later in this chapter. Other than that, sending files between Macs and PCs via email is no different from sending them from one PC to another the same way.

But what do you do about files too large to email? You can use a go-between site like www.yousendit.com. It's a really clever system – you upload your file to the YouSendIt site, and at the same time an email is sent to the recipient with a link to download it. Files remain available for a few days – long enough for the other person to fetch them at their leisure. This service is free for light personal use and it has a huge 100Mb file limit (businesses have to pay, but get larger file and usage limits). It's unlikely you'll ever

As long as the file's no larger than around 5Mb, the easiest way to send it to someone else is as an email attachment.

need to send anything larger than this and, if you do, use one of the
following methods.

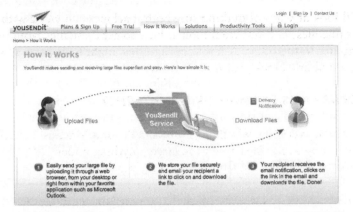

You can send files up to 100Mb in size via the Internet using the free transfer service at www.yousendit.com

Author insight

Email is the easiest way to send files to PC owners. Just about
everyone uses broadband these days, so it's cheap, fast and
effective for files of around 5Mb or less. If they're bigger than
that, use a free file transfer service like www.yousendit.com.
Post is so passé...

If you've got a batch of files to send over the Internet, it's
worth compressing them into a zip archive first. It's not
that it saves any space – many file formats like JPEGs, for
example, are compressed already – but it means you're
sending a single attachment and not half a dozen.

BURN A CD

When you insert a blank CD into your Mac's CD-ROM drive, its
icon appears on the Desktop and you can copy files to it as you
would any other drive – up to the CD's maximum 650–700Mb limit.

When you've copied the files across, you then burn the CD, a
process which takes a few minutes. Once that's done, you can eject

the CD and send it to the other person. CDs are cheap, so while it might be inconvenient for it to be lost or damaged in transit, it's hardly going to break the bank. And given the low cost, you don't need to worry about getting the other person to send it back, either.

Author insight

You can still use CDs and DVDs for data transfer between computers but they're fast becoming obsolete. They're slow and tiresome to create and their capacity is limited by today's standards. Their only advantage is their low cost, which can be useful if you don't expect to get them back.

USE A USB FLASH DRIVE

CDs are cheap and disposable, but you can only use them once and they're comparatively slow for saving and accessing data. They also have a limited capacity. You could use a DVD instead, but these are also a little slow and inconvenient to prepare, too. CDs and DVDs are good for sending data away, but they're less convenient when you just want to carry files yourself from one computer to another. For this a USB flash drive is ideal. These are just an inch or so long and plug straight into a USB socket. The icon appears on the Desktop and you can use the Finder to copy files and folders across.

USB flash drives come in various capacities, and they're now remarkably cheap. In the UK, a 2Gb drive will typically cost around £5, and you can get them in capacities up to 16Gb or even 32Gb. They offer much higher capacities than CDs, much faster data transfer and they can be re-used indefinitely. They're perfect for carrying files between office and home, for example, or between home and school.

EXTERNAL HARD DISKS

The next step up is a portable external hard disk. These too plug into a USB socket, and this is where they get their power – there's no need for a separate power cable. This makes them very convenient for carrying around in a briefcase, say.

External hard disks come in varying capacities, starting at around 250Gb and going all the way up to 500Gb or even 1Tb (1000Gb). They're perfect for transferring files between Macs and PCs (though they do have to use PC FAT32 formatting) and they're also useful for keeping backups of your important files.

Nowadays, then, it's just as easy to swap files between Macs and PCs as it is between one PC and another.

Author insight

If you have to work on both a Mac and a PC, try keeping your work files on a portable external disk drive and using software (or at least file formats) which can be used on both. Then you can just plug the disk drive into whichever machine you happen to be using at the time.

8.2 Joining a network

There is another way to swap files between a Mac and a PC and that's by connecting them on a network. You can set up a small network from scratch to link a PC and a Mac, or you can connect the Mac to an existing PC network. Corporate networks in large offices are complex things and you'd need to check with the network administrator to find out what you'd need to do. In the home, though, it's much simpler. A home or small office network will consist of two or more machines connected to a router. The router handles all the data traffic between these computers. (We met routers in Chapter 5.)

When a Mac (or a PC) is on a network, it can see the other machines on the network, but can only access those folders which the users of those machines have specifically set up for sharing. It's the same on the Mac – the other computers on the network can only see your shared folders, not the entire contents of your hard disk.

The Mac's online Help system explains the basics of networking in more detail than we have the space for here. The important thing to understand is that connecting to a PC network isn't just possible, it's easy.

In Leopard and Snow Leopard, the Finder Sidebar has a Shared section which lists any other computers on the network. You can click on any of these machines to see what shared folders exist on each, and then click on these folders to access the contents.

It's important to set up user names and passwords for shared folders as a matter of habit. If these are required for any of the computers you access over the network, you'll be asked to type them into a dialog.

8.3 Common file types

There are many ways to transfer files between Macs and PCs, but you also need to make sure that each machine can make sense of the other's files. This used to be quite a problem, and there were all sorts of third-party file-conversion programs on the market. Now, thankfully, none of this is necessary any more.

The fact is that many files are now of a standard type that can be read by both machines. For example, digital photos are usually in the JPEG file format, or sometimes the TIFF format or the RAW format used by some professional cameras. These files are all freely interchangeable between Macs and PCs. So are music files in the MP3 format. iTunes uses its own format, admittedly, but can be configured to record CD tracks as MP3s. As the iPod and iTunes have gained in popularity, though, an increasing number of devices support the Mac's AAC format anyway.

Sometimes people compress files which are to be sent as email attachments. This is almost always done using the Zip compressed file format on the PC, and the Mac supports Zip files directly too.

The Mac uses the same .zip compressed file format as Windows PCs. You can create zip archives directly in the Finder.

Ch08-Working with PCs.zip

And even if you're using Pages, Keynote and Numbers on the Mac where your work colleagues are using Microsoft Word, PowerPoint and Excel, it's not a problem because the Mac's iWork applications can open these file types directly. When you save your work, choose a format that Microsoft Office can read – like the Word doc format, for example, when saving a Pages document, while in Numbers you should export spreadsheets in the Excel format. (In iWork 09 you use the Export rather than the Save As command.)

Where the same software is being used on both computers, there isn't a problem. Microsoft Office users can swap files from Mac to PC and back again without a hitch. It's the same when you're working with photo-montages in Adobe Photoshop or professional page layouts in InDesign.

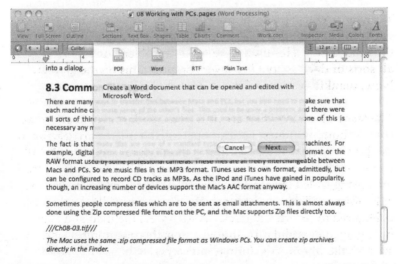

If you and the other person are using different programs, you'll need to make sure you save your files in a format that the other person's software can read.

Where the applications are different, you simply need to find a common file format that both applications understand. This happens when you're swapping files between PCs, too, if they don't both have the same software. It's difficult to generalize about this because each set of circumstances is different, but there's almost always a way of finding a format for transferring data between two different programs. For example, database programs all use their own specific file formats, but you can use a simple comma separated values (CSV) file format that both programs understand to swap data between them. Where there's a will there's a way!

For the most part, transferring files between Macs and PCs is no more difficult than transferring them between one Mac and another or one PC and another. There is, however, one technical difference between Macs and PCs you should be aware of...

FILE TYPES AND EXTENSIONS

With both Macs and PCs you can simply double-click a file to open it. The computer knows which program to launch to do this because that information is embedded in the file. But it's done in different ways.

Windows users will know that files have three-letter extensions (sometimes four letters now) which identify the file type, such as '.jpg' for JPEG files or '.doc' for Microsoft Word documents. These extensions may be hidden, depending on the view options chosen in Windows Explorer, but they're still there and they're vital because Windows needs them to identify the file type and hence the program needed to open them.

Macs don't need file extensions. The creator information is embedded invisibly in the file data.

If you get a file from a PC it will have a three-letter extension on the end, but the Mac tolerates this perfectly well. What can happen, though, is that if you create a file on the Mac and omit the three-letter extension on the end, when you send it to a PC owner they can't open it. Without the extension, the PC won't know what sort of file it is and what to do with it.

One solution is to add the extension manually in Windows. The other is to make sure you always add extensions to filenames on the Mac. It's good practice, because you never know when these files might be needed on a PC.

Don't worry, though – you don't have to memorize dozens of file type extensions and type them in manually. Most Mac applications will add them automatically when you save the file – if not, there's usually an option you can select which activates this.

Windows PCs use three-letter file extensions to identify file types. The Mac doesn't need these but displays them anyway to remain compatible with PCs.

Author insight

Most file formats are 'platform-agnostic'. It's the software which created them that's important, not the machine they're being used on.

TEST

1 *We suggest five different ways of getting files to other people. What are they?*

2 *CDs and DVDs were once the most popular choice for large-scale data transfers, but what are their weaknesses today?*

3 *What are the advantages of USB flash drives?*

4 *Where does a portable external hard disk get its power?*

5 *Can both Macs and PCs use the same external hard disk?*

6 *Is your data safe on a network?*

7 *What do you do if you want to share a file with a PC owner using different software?*

8 *Macs and PCs now use the same compressed file format – what is it?*

9 *Why does the Mac display file extensions if it doesn't use them?*

10 *What can you do if you accidentally send someone using a PC a file without its extension?*

9

iPhoto

In this chapter you will learn:

- *about iPhoto*
- *how to import photos from a camera*
- *how to view your photos*
- *how to organize and share photos*
- *about ratings, comments and keywords*
- *about Albums and Smart Albums*
- *how to edit and print photos*
- *how to create slideshows*

9.1 What is iPhoto?

iPhoto is supplied pre-installed with all new Macs. It's a photo cataloguing program which can also edit and enhance pictures, print them out and create greetings cards, calendars, photo books, slideshows and web albums. It's part of iLife 09, the latest version of Apple's lifestyle software suite, which also includes iMovie, iDVD, iWeb and GarageBand.

iPhoto Library

iPhoto is easy to use but it's also very powerful. It displays all your photos in a single, searchable library, and can also organize them into individual albums. It can accommodate up to 250,000 photos, so the size of your photo collection is more likely to be limited by the amount of hard disk space you have available, not iPhoto itself.

9.2 How iPhoto works

Earlier versions of iPhoto imported your photos into an iPhoto Library folder in the Pictures folder on your Mac. iPhoto now creates a single Library file, which is a little less confusing. This file contains the photos, keywords, editing adjustments, albums and everything else you create in iPhoto.

There is one option you should be aware of before you import large numbers of images, though. By default, these are copied into the iPhoto Library, so you'll end up with duplicates of your photos, which could fill up your hard disk prematurely. This is unlikely to be a problem with the latest Macs, but can be an issue with older models with smaller hard disks.

By default, iPhoto copies your pictures into your library, but you can set it to refer to them in their existing location.

It is possible to get iPhoto 09 to reference your existing photos in their current location.

1 Use the **iPhoto > Preferences** menu command.
2 In the **Preferences** dialog, click the **Advanced** button.
3 De-select the box labelled **Copy items to the iPhoto Library**.

iPhoto will still create a Library file, but this time it will simply keep a record of where the photos are located. In use, iPhoto will work in just the same way. The one thing you have to be careful about, though, is moving any of your photos later using the Finder, because iPhoto may lose track of where they are.

Author insight

iPhoto is fine for amateur photographers, but professionals will need something with a bit more power. The next step up is Aperture, which brings much more advanced editing and cataloguing tools. The good news is that Aperture can import iPhoto libraries directly.

9.3 Importing photos

There are two ways of importing photos into your Library. Choose the one that makes most sense to you.

IMPORT PHOTOS ALREADY ON YOUR HARD DISK

This assumes the photos have already been transferred from the digital camera. You can transfer photos from your camera to your Mac's hard disk either by connecting the camera to the Mac using the camera's USB cable, or by taking out the memory card and inserting it into a memory card reader plugged into the Mac. If you have installed the camera maker's software, it may attempt to transfer the pictures from the camera automatically. This isn't always a good thing because it may not always be obvious where the software is going to save the photos. It's best to plan your own system of folders for storing your photo collection, using the Finder.

1 Cancel any automatic download and then quit. You should find an icon for the camera on the Desktop.
2 Double-click this icon to open it, then double-click the folders inside.
3 Locate your photos and drag them across to your computer manually.
4 Start iPhoto, open the **File** menu, choose the **Import to Library** command, locate the photos and import them.

You can import photos which have already been copied from your camera on to your Mac's hard disk.

IMPORT PHOTOS FROM YOUR CAMERA/MEMORY CARD

To download photos directly from the camera:

1 Start iPhoto, then plug in your camera.
2 iPhoto should detect your camera automatically and switch to Import view, ready to copy across the photos.
3 If not, or you're importing pictures from a memory card reader, use the **File > Import to Library** command and look for the camera or memory card reader's icon on the Desktop.

If you connect a digital camera while iPhoto is running it will detect it automatically and offer to import any photos on the camera.

If this is the route you want to follow, remember what we said earlier about the iPhoto preferences. Make sure iPhoto is copying the files into the Library. Otherwise, when you remove the card, iPhoto won't be able to locate them any more.

The import process may take anything from a few seconds to several minutes, depending on the number of photos.

Once the import process is complete, you'll see your photos have been added to the Library as a new event. This is a new feature introduced in iPhoto 08 – previously, photos were imported in rolls.

Events are Apple's attempt to simplify the way we browse ever-larger collections of photos. Each event is represented by an icon – but not an ordinary icon. If you move the mouse pointer from left to right across it, you'll see that you can skim through all the photos in the event, seeing what's there without actually having to open the event itself.

In iPhoto, sets of photos are automatically split into 'Events' when you import them.

Author insight

There are other ways of organizing your photos besides iPhoto. Google's Picasa is very good and you can now get it in a Mac version. The big advantage of iPhoto, though, is that it stores all your photos in a single library file rather than in dozens of different folders.

9.4 Viewing and browsing photos

Now let's take a closer look at the iPhoto interface. Running vertically down the left-hand side of the screen is the Source list. At the top, in the Library section, you can click on Events to view your photos as Events, or Photos to view them as one long, continuous list. In iPhoto 09, the latest version, there are two further items: Faces and Places.

Like other Mac applications, iPhoto uses a sidebar, this time to display its photo Source list. This includes events and any albums you create.

▶ **Faces** *uses a new face-detection system which can pick out human faces and, when you put a name to the face, it can automatically recognize the same people elsewhere in your iPhoto library. It does take a little 'training' – for a while, it will keep popping up photos and ask you to identify the people in them – and the initial scan does take some time, but it could be a useful feature for keeping track of all your photos of friends and family.*

▶ **Places** *uses 'geotagging', which is a way of embedding the location* *where a shot was taken into the image. Some cameras have GPS receivers which can do this automatically, but you can also add this information in iPhoto by 'pinning' photos to a map. The Places feature is quite neat if you want to show people an itinerary of your journey or look up photos by location visually.*

Below this is the **Recent** section. This contains a button to display the last event you looked at, the last 12 months' worth of pictures, the last import (the batch you added most recently), flagged images and a Trash icon.

To flag a photo, click on it in the main window to select it and then click the Flag button at the bottom of the screen. When you click the Flag button in the Recent section of the panel on the left, all the photos you've flagged are displayed. You might flag photos that you want to come back to later, or those that are going to need some enhancement, or pictures you want to consider for a photo book or web album.

When you create your first Album, a new Album section is added to the Source list, with your new album in it. Any smart albums (see section 9.8) that you create are shown here, too. You can leave these as a single list, or organize them into folders.

If you have a MobileMe account (this used to be called .Mac), there may be a section for your MobileMe online photo galleries at the bottom too.

9.5 Creating albums

You can browse through your photos using the events created automatically by iPhoto, but it's likely that you'll prefer to organize them manually, especially where you want to combine photos taken on different locations – you might want to create a Birthdays album, for example.

There are two ways to create an album:

1 Select the photos you want in the main window.
2 To select more than one, click on the first in a series and then [**Shift**]-click on the last to select both photos and all of those in between.
3 If there are gaps between the photos you want, [**Command**]-click on each photo you want to select.
4 Drag the photos on to a blank area in the Source list. A new album is created with these, and its name is highlighted ready for you to type in a name of your own.

Alternatively, start by creating the album using File > New Album. Now drag the photos you want into this album either individually or several at a time.

9.6 Using keywords and comments

You may find that albums provide you with all the organizational tools you need. Sometimes, though, you will find that photos don't fit neatly into a single Album, or that you forget which album contains the photo you want. This is where keywords are useful.

Keywords are individual words or phrases which can be embedded in digital photos so that programs like iPhoto can search for particular images.

To display iPhoto's keywords, open the Window menu and choose the **Show Keywords** command, or use the [**Command**]-[**K**] shortcut. (In earlier versions of iPhoto, keywords were displayed in a panel in the bottom left-hand corner of the window.)

The Keywords palette may already contain some keywords, depending on whether any of the pictures imported already had keywords assigned by another program. But you can add your own. To do this, click the Edit Keywords button at the bottom. Keywords can also be typed in directly below the photo in the main window.

The Keywords palette has a separate Quick Group section at the top for commonly-used keywords with their own single-letter shortcuts, and the full list of keywords is displayed below this.

In earlier versions of iPhoto you could find pictures which had particular keywords by clicking the keyword in the panel. From iPhoto 08 onwards, the Keywords palette is just for keyword management. To search for photos you now use the unified Search box at the bottom of the window.

iPhoto's searches are amazingly fast, as you'll discover, but you may get more photos than you bargained for. How do you narrow down the search? Well, if you type more than one keyword into the Search box, iPhoto will only find photos that match both keywords.

Keywords aren't the only way to tag photos with information. You can also type in freeform comments using the Info panel displayed in the bottom left-hand corner. (If this isn't visible, click the 'i' button below the Source list.) Use the comments area to type in more detailed descriptions of your photos. When you use the Search box, iPhoto will also use these descriptions to help you find the photos you want.

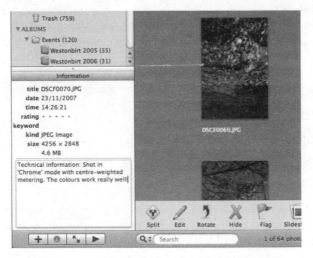

The Comments panel enables you to type in longer descriptions for individual photographs.

9.7 Using ratings

You'll notice that this Information panel also allows you to type in star ratings between one and five for photos and these can also be entered by clicking the row of star buttons below each photo in the main window. It's up to you how you choose to rate pictures, and whether you bother at all, but ratings can be useful later on as you try to pick out your very best photos from an ever-expanding library. For example, you could create an album for your last holiday and then rate each photo individually. Once you've done that, select the album to display your holiday shots, then open the View menu and choose the Sort Photos command and Rating (make sure you select the Descending option from the Sort menu, though, or you'll get the lowest-rated pictures showing up first).

If you want to see the star ratings underneath each photo, open the View menu and choose My Rating.

Ratings are also useful if you decide to use smart albums, which we'll be looking at next.

If you give your pictures star ratings you make it much easier to find your best ones later on.

9.8 Smart albums

Ordinary albums are a great way to organize your photos, but they require a good deal of manual upkeep. What if there was some way of getting iPhoto to create and maintain albums automatically? There is, and it's called smart albums.

Smart albums are automatically filled with photos that have specific properties. For example, you might want a smart album that displays all your holiday photos.

Before you start, set up any keywords that you will be using.

1 Open the **File** menu and choose **New Smart Album**.
2 Choose a name for the smart album and then adjust its search conditions. This sounds more technical than it is.
3 Using the pop-up menu, choose **Keyword** as the condition and choose 'is' from the pop-up to its right. The third pop-up, far right, should now display the list of keywords applied to your photos and 'holiday' should be amongst them. This is a search criterion and it has three parts: the type of data you're looking for, whether it's an exact value or within a certain range, and what this data is.
4 That's it. All done. The new smart album will automatically display all photos with the 'holiday' keyword. As long as you remember to add this keyword to all your holiday shots in future, the smart album will update automatically.

Smart albums are smarter even than that, though. You can set up more than one condition (criterion) to narrow the conditions. For example, the second condition could be that the rating is 5 stars. Now the album will only display your 5-star holiday shots. The other advantage of smart albums over the ordinary sort is that if in the future you decide to change the keywords or the ratings for some of your photos, any smart albums will, again, update automatically.

This smart album picks out all the 5-star photos in a 'Trannie' event (photos shot on transparency film, just in case you were wondering).

9.9 Editing photos

iPhoto is great for collecting and organizing photos, then, but what can it do about fixing up photo failures and generally enhancing your pictures?

1 To edit a photo, open the View menu and choose Full Screen, or use the Full Screen button in the bottom left-hand corner of the iPhoto window (two opposed arrows, next to the 'i' button).

2　In full screen mode, if you move the pointer to the bottom of
   the screen, a strip of image-editing controls will appear. These
   include Rotate, Crop and Straighten tools, a quick-fix Enhance
   button, a Red-eye button, Retouch, Effects and an Adjust
   button.
3　If you click the Adjust button, this will display iPhoto's full set
   of image adjustment tools. They're surprisingly powerful and,
   while they're not on quite the same level as a proper image-
   editing program like Adobe Photoshop or Elements, they are
   still more than adequate for correcting common image flaws,
   and the Effects button reveals a selection of attractive pre-set
   image effects like black and white, sepia and more.

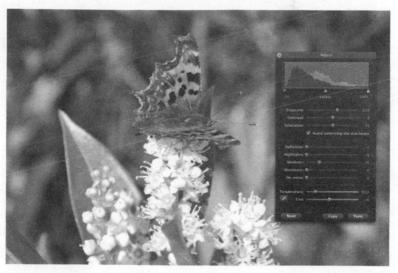

iPhoto has a wide range of tools for enhancing photos and all these adjustments can be reversed later
on if need be.

In older versions of iPhoto, if you changed a picture, iPhoto would
save the new version, but also keep the old one in case you needed
to go back to it. In iPhoto 08 and 09, the original image is never
actually modified. Instead, the changes you make are stored within
iPhoto as a series of instructions. If you open the photo in future, the
positions of the adjustment sliders are just as you left them, so that
you can carry on changing your mind about how best to enhance

a photo without ever committing yourself to permanent changes to the image. It's called non-destructive editing, and it's a new way of editing photos that's starting to appear in other programs, too.

Author insight

iPhoto has a range of image adjustment tools, but before you use any of them, try the automatic enhancement button. This can magically transform a picture in a single step, and the changes it applies are displayed in the adjustments panel, so you can easily undo or modify them if they've gone too far.

9.10 Printing photos

Now collecting thousands of photos on your computer is a pretty dry and dusty pastime unless you find some way of sharing them with other people.

The simplest and most traditional method is to print them out, and there are lots of really good low-cost inkjet printers out there which can produce photographic prints every bit as good as those you'd get from a conventional photo lab.

1 To print a picture from within iPhoto, simply select it in the main window and press the Print button at the bottom.
2 This displays a dialog where you can choose the print style from a list on the left (Standard, Contact Sheet, Framed). To the right is a preview of how the photo will look with the current settings.
3 In the area below, you need to make sure the correct printer is selected and that the paper type, size and print quality are set correctly too. With inkjet printers it's essential to use proper photo paper and to tell the printer that's what's being used. If you don't, the picture quality will be badly affected because the amount of ink the printer delivers must be tailored precisely to each paper type.

4 To output a photo, press the Print button and choose the page size and photo layout required.

9.11 Creating slideshows

The alternative to prints is a slideshow. At one time you wouldn't have thought about getting friends and family to gather round a computer screen, but with today's larger, higher-resolution displays – and particularly the excellent iMac displays – there's no reason not to. The chances are your computer's display is now not a whole lot smaller than the TV in the corner of the lounge.

Slideshows are easy to set up in iPhoto.

1 It's best to first create an album containing the pictures you want to show.
2 Click the album to select it, then click the **Slideshow** button at the bottom of the screen.

3 iPhoto will display the first picture and, underneath, a range of slideshow settings. You can have a lot of fun playing with the slide delay, the Ken Burns effect and even adding your own music track, but for now just press the **Play** button to get a feel for how it works.

4 For a much more professional look, create a new Slideshow album – open the **New** menu, choose **New Album,** and then choose **Slideshow** from the list of options.

5 You'll now get a much more advanced set of slideshow options including some wonderful-looking pre-designed slideshow Themes. These slideshow albums are saved in your iPhoto library, so you can come back to them whenever you like.

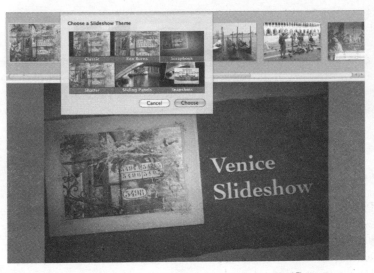

iPhoto can create fantastic-looking slideshows, thanks to its selection of pre-designed Themes.

Author insight

iPhoto slideshows are a great way to show your pictures to your friends or family, and you can apply a number of very professional-looking design themes. You can even export your slideshows as movies.

9.12 Cards, books and calendars

To the right of the Slideshow button at the bottom of the iPhoto window are buttons for creating books, calendars and cards. This is another way of sharing your photos, this time by turning them into personalized gift items. In each case you can choose a template and customize it with your own photos, messages and information. The options are really quite impressive... but how do you print these out?

These options tie in with Apple's own online printing services. Many photo lab sites already offer gift items like these, and iPhoto is clearly tapping into this market. But you don't have to order books, calendars and cards online. You can print the pages on your own printer, if you like, and you might well want to do this if you're simply interested in trying these things out.

In the long run, getting gift items like these made commercially does make a certain amount of sense, particularly with photo books. You could print out the pages individually, but you wouldn't be able to bind them as effectively or as professionally as an online photo lab.

9.13 Creating web albums

iPhoto can also publish your photos as web albums, and there are three ways of doing this: (a) by publishing them to a personal web gallery, though for this you need a MobileMe account; (b) by sending them to the iWeb application that comes with the Mac; (c) by exporting simple web page layouts which you can then upload yourself to whatever web host you want to use.

These web galleries are like those you can create using Yahoo! and other sites with photo album features. But where Yahoo! and others let you choose and upload your photos from within your Internet browser, it's obviously an advantage to be able to do it from within iPhoto instead, if that's the tool you use to organize your pictures.

And this means you will need a web host of some description, whether it's one you choose yourself or an Apple MobileMe account.

A MobileMe account is the simplest option, but it's not free. Currently in the UK they come with an annual subscription of around £59. It might sound a lot if you're used to things on the Internet being free, but you do get a lot for your money, and you can find out more about MobileMe and what it offers in Chapter 14.

One advantage of using the MobileMe service is that creating a web gallery is easy. You just create and name an album to store the photos you want to include, select all the photos in the album and click the MobileMe button at the bottom of the window. iPhoto uses the album name as the web gallery name and asks you who you want to be able to see the photos (the online Help explains the privacy settings). Now you click the Publish button. The photos are then uploaded to the web gallery (this may take a few minutes, depending on the number of photos). You can click a link to visit the published site when the upload is complete, and send an email inviting others to come and look at it, all within iPhoto.

There's more, though. When visitors take a look at your web gallery, what they get is not just another photo gallery website – it's a rich, interactive experience! Galleries can be viewed in four modes: Grid (an array of thumbnails), Mosaic (one big image with thumbnails alongside), Carousel (you move a slider to 'spin' photos through the viewer) and slideshow. It's also possible to adjust the settings so that friends and relatives can download the photos and even upload their own.

Web galleries published in this fashion are shown in iPhoto's source list so that you can examine them, add or remove photos and republish them as required.

We mentioned that you can also export sets of photos to iWeb. Here's how.

1 Select the photos and click the **iWeb** button at the bottom of the iPhoto window.

2 You can choose between two templates: Photo Page and Blog. This is a good route to follow if you've already used iWeb to set up your own web page and you want to integrate your photo albums with this.

3 To export a simple web page which can be uploaded manually to another server, select the photos and use the **File > Export** command.

4 This displays the Export Photos dialog, which has a Web Page section. Here you can choose the title of the web page, the number and size of the thumbnail images and the size of the photos themselves. This generates all the files needed for uploading and displaying the album. All you need now is instructions from your Internet service provider or web host on how and where the files should be uploaded.

iPhoto's online MobileMe galleries are quite stunning, though you can only create them if you invest in a MobileMe account.

Author insight

Want to get your photos online? You don't have to sign up to MobileMe to do it. iPhoto 09 can also publish direct to your Facebook profile or a Flickr account.

TEST

1 *Does iPhoto leave your photos where they are or does it move them?*

2 *What does 'Faces' in iPhoto 09 do?*

3 *What's 'geotagging'?*

4 *What's the difference between an album and a smart album?*

5 *What's a keyword?*

6 *Can you suggest two uses for ratings?*

7 *How do you edit photos?*

8 *What does 'non-destructive' editing mean?*

9 *You can create quick slideshows with the Slideshow button on the bottom toolbar, but there's another way which creates permanent slideshows with professional designs. What is it?*

10 *There are three ways to create online photo albums with iPhoto. What are they?*

10

Using iTunes

In this chapter you will learn:
- *what iTunes can do*
- *how to copy audio CDs to your iTunes library*
- *where iTunes gets CD track information*
- *how to organize your music*
- *how to create playlists*
- *how to create audio CDs*
- *about iTunes and iPods*
- *about the iTunes store*
- *about podcasts*
- *about Internet radio*

10.1 What is iTunes?

iTunes is a way of building and organizing your music collection on your Mac. If you want to hear a favourite piece of music, you no longer have to go looking for the CD it's stored on and find the right track on the CD. Instead, you can use the tools within iTunes to find specific artists, tracks or albums in an instant, even when your Library consists of thousands of tracks (iTunes calls them songs).

It's also the tool used to synchronize mobile Mac devices like the iPhone and iPad, and not just for music files but photos and apps too.

Your Mac can store thousands of tracks because they're recorded in a compressed format which doesn't noticeably affect their audio quality, but which greatly reduces the size of the music files. The music on an audio CD might take up around 600Mb of storage space on the CD, but once it's imported into iTunes the same tracks might only take up 60Mb. These tracks are stored in the Music folder (see Chapter 2 for more information on how and where files are stored on the Mac). If more than one person is using the Mac, then each user will have their own Music folder.

If you've used Windows Media Player on a PC, you'll find iTunes very similar in terms of what it does, even though it actually looks quite different. You can use iTunes to enjoy your music as is, using your Mac as a kind of hi-fi system (you can get plug-in speaker systems which provide excellent quality), or you can use it to create your own audio CD compilations – handy for the car, perhaps, or your domestic hi-fi system.

What's significant about iTunes is the way it's integrated with other Apple software. For example, if you're creating a presentation in Keynote, you can add an audio soundtrack directly from your iTunes library. Mostly, though, people use iTunes in conjunction with an iPod, creating playlists of favourite tracks in iTunes and

iTunes can store your whole music library on your Mac and find any track you want in an instant.

then synchronizing them with the iPod so that they get to hear their favourite music on the move.

Music can be imported in one of two ways. The usual way is to copy it from audio CDs, but it is also possible to buy music digitally by paying for it and downloading it from the iTunes store. We'll look at the iTunes store later in this chapter, but for now we'll look at the way most people will get their music into iTunes – by copying it from CDs.

10.2 Copying CDs to your Library

Like many tasks on the Mac, importing an audio CD is so simple that it'll bring a smile to your face. Just insert the CD into the slot, wait a few moments for the Mac to mount the CD and you should find that iTunes starts automatically. It will then display a list of the tracks on the CD, together with the artist and album name, and to the left of each track is a checkbox with a tick in it. When you click the Import CD button at the bottom right of the iTunes window, it will import all the tracks which have been ticked – this is your opportunity to deselect any tracks you don't want, although it's simpler to import them all and make up playlists later which contain only those you like listening to.

Wait a minute. How does iTunes know what all the tracks are called? This information isn't on the CD. Ah, but each CD sold has its own unique identifying code, and iTunes looks this code up on an online Gracenote database which carries track listings for every CD on sale. If you look carefully at the iTunes display while it's scanning the CD, you'll see it accessing this database.

This will only work, of course, if your Mac is connected to the Internet when you insert the CD. With a broadband connection, this will be on all the time, and the data will be retrieved automatically. If you're unable to connect to the Internet when you copy a CD, it's possible to look up track names later on when you do have a connection. To do this, first select the track. Next, open the **Advanced** menu and choose **Get CD Track Names**.

If you copy a CD which isn't on the Gracenote database, you can type in track, artist and album names manually. To do this, click a name to select it, wait a moment, then click it again to make it editable (if your clicks are too close together, the Mac will interpret them as a double-click and simply start playing the track). Now use the information on the CD inlay to fill in the names.

In fact this is your chance to give something back to the world of music! Once you've finished entering the CD information, open the **Advanced** menu and choose **Submit CD Track Names** menu command to upload them to the Gracenote database.

Importing music is simple. When you insert a CD, iTunes looks up the album and track names on the Internet and offers to import them into your library.

Author insight

The iTunes store is a great way to buy music, but there's still a lot to be said for ordering a CD and then copying it. It takes longer, but at the end of it you've still got the physical disc the music came from rather than just a bunch of digital files.

10.3 Organizing your music

The iTunes interface can look a little daunting for first-timers. Where Windows Media Player puts on a very pretty face, iTunes looks like just what it is, a music database. But don't worry, it's all very straightforward. And before long you really start to appreciate this direct approach.

The iTunes window has two parts. On the left is a vertical sidebar with a series of sections. iTunes is updated pretty regularly by Apple, so these may have changed by the time you read this. At the time of writing (iTunes 9.2.1), these include the following:

The Store, which is the iTunes Store, where you can get music, movies and apps.

A new 'Shared' section which enables you to share your music with other Mac devices in the house.

The new 'Genius' section, which tries to build a themed playlist based around a track you've selected, or 'Mixes' based on specific genres.

Under 'Devices' you'll find the currently inserted CD (if any) or an iPod, if you've got one connected.

The 'Playlists' section lists all the custom playlists you've created (collections of your favourite tracks) together with Smart Playlists, which are created automatically based on your ratings and other information. We'll look at playlists in more detail in the next section, and some of the other items (podcasts, radio) at the end.

The Library section has entries for music, movies, TV shows, podcasts, any apps you've downloaded for iPhone or iPad, and Internet radio stations.

The point is that when you click any of the items in the sidebar, you see all the relevant tracks in the main panel on the right. And it's the organization of these tracks and the way that they're displayed which we'll explain next.

In the iTunes toolbar there are three view option buttons, just to the left of the search box. These activate the List, Album and Cover Flow views...

LIST VIEW

In List view, the tracks are displayed in rows and the information for each – the Name, Time, Artist and so on – is arranged in columns. You can change the order in which they're displayed.

Name	Time	Artist	Album
☑ Don Giovanni	6:49	Crudele – Non mi dir	Opera Gala
☑ Von Weber	3:50	Der Freischutz – Ko...	Opera Gala
☑ Von Weber	11:04	Der Freischutz – Ov...	Opera Gala
☑ Von Weber	2:52	Der Freischutz – W...	Opera Gala
☑ Wagner	8:03	Die Walk|Rie – Act ...	Classic CD Issue 44
☑ Die Zauberflote	3:54	Dies Bildnis ist bez...	Opera Gala
☑ Madama Butterfly	3:02	Dovunque al mond...	Opera gala
☑ Le Nozze di Figaro	7:22	E Dusanna nom vie...	Opera Gala
☑ Madama Butterfly	1:05	Ed e bella la sposa?	Opera gala
☑ Otello –– Act 2, "Ora e per sempre addio"	2:26	Enrico Caruso	Classic CD 47
☑ Beethoven	7:35	Fidelio – Abscheuli...	Opera Gala
☑ Beethoven	10:28	Fidelio – Gott! Welc...	Opera Gala
☑ Beethoven	6:25	Fidelio – Overture	Opera Gala
☑ Jour a Jour – Anon	3:40	Gothic Voices	Classic CD – Disc 32
☑ Humperdinck	8:09	Hansel und Gretel ...	Opera Gala
☑ Budapest	10:05	Jethro Tull	Crest Of A Knave
☑ Teseo, Act 3 – finale, Sibillando	3:43	Jones (Medea); Les ...	Classic CD 29
☑ Requiem – Dies irae; Tuba mirum	5:31	Konzertvereinigung...	Classic CD Issue 42...
☑ Neon Lights	8:54	Kraftwerk	The Man Machine
☑ The Man Machine	5:32	Kraftwerk	The Man Machine
☑ Symphony No. 6 in E minor – first mov	8:29	London Symphony ...	Classic CD 29
☑ The Masses Against The Classes	3:24	Manic Street Preach...	Masses Against Th...
☑ Puccini	8:51	Manon Lescaut – O...	Opera Gala
☑ Chasing Sheep Is Best Left To Shepherds	2:35	Michael Nyman	The Draughtsman's...
☑ The Disposition Of The Linen	4:49	Michael Nyman	The Draughtsman's...
☑ Queen Of The Night	6:10	Michael Nyman	The Draughtsman's...
☑ Don Carlo –– Act 1, "E lui! desso l'infante!"	8:01	Michael Sylvester (...	Classic CD 36

In list view, your tracks are shown in a database-style table – the information in each track is shown in the different columns, and the more organized you are in putting details into this, the easier it will be to find tracks.

For example, if you click on the Album column, the tracks will be arranged alphabetically by album name. See the little arrow to the right? You can click this to swap between Ascending (A–Z) and Descending order (Z–A).

So much for sorting tracks – but how do you find specific tracks out of a collection of thousands? Simply type the name (or an artist, or album name) into the Search box at the top right of the window. In an instant it will list the tracks, you're looking for.

ALBUM VIEW

List view is the most useful for experienced iTunes users, but it may put many newcomers off because it looks like a database program. Album view is more logical for those who still think of their music in terms of the CDs it's stored on. Here, tracks are grouped by album, though this display format only really works if you have the album artwork too – an image of the album cover, in other words.

Album view will make the most sense to those used to sorting through a conventional CD collection.

Artwork is available from the iTunes store, and is downloaded automatically if you buy music from the store. You can also download artwork for existing tracks from the iTunes store by opening the **Advanced** menu and choosing the **Get Album Artwork** command. However, this does require an iTunes account, which means supplying your credit card details in advance of any purchases you might make.

COVER FLOW VIEW

This restriction also applies to the Cover Flow view. This is a very smart-looking display mode where you can flick through your albums (album artwork, that is) to find the album you want.

It is possible to add your own artwork to albums, but it means scanning in CD inlays or record sleeves, and it's more trouble than most of us are likely to want to go to. So unless you buy into the whole iTunes store idea, which is the place to get the artwork, you're better off using iTunes in its simple List view.

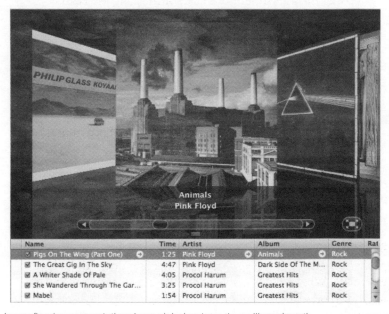

In cover flow view you can spin through your cds by dragging on the scrollbar underneath.

10.4 Creating playlists

We've explained how your music tracks are displayed and how you can sort them in the order you want and find specific tracks, but this isn't much use if you just want to sit back and listen to a few favourites played in a particular order. That's what playlists are for.

To create a playlist:

1 Click the '+' button in the bottom left-hand corner of the iTunes window.

2 A new, 'untitled' playlist is created, ready for you to type in a name.

3 Click **Music** in the Library section at the top of the panel.

4 Find the tracks you want in your Library either by sorting them by album or artist, or by using the Search box.

5 Once you've found a track you want, just drag it on to the playlist. Do this with all the other tracks you want until your playlist is finished.

6 Click the playlist title to display its contents in the main window. Is the order wrong? Just drag tracks up and down the list to change the order.

7 Have you missed a track out? Go back to Music, find the track and drag it on to the playlist.

Playlists are useful when you want to listen to your favourite tracks on your Mac, but that's not all. They're also perfect for creating compilation audio CDs for playback on conventional CD players, and they're particularly useful when transferring music to an iPod. iPods don't have as large a storage capacity as your Mac, so you'll probably need to prune your music collection down to its bare essentials. What's more, you can't manage and organize music on your iPod – all the organization (like creating playlists) has to be done on the Mac.

iTunes also offers smart playlists, and these can be a lot of fun, though they are far from essential.

Let's say you want a Wagner playlist but you can't be bothered to search through your whole Library for all your Wagnerian operas.

1 Open the **File** menu and choose the **New Smart Playlist** command.
2 This displays a dialog where you can specify your smart search criteria. We could just choose Artist from the menu and type 'Wagner' into the box. It might work, but there will be many tracks where the artist is actually the performer and 'Wagner' may appear only in the track name, or even just the album title.
3 To get round this you can add more search 'criteria' by clicking the '+' button to the right of the first one.

We won't go into any more detail here, but hopefully the idea is a little clearer now. And it'll become clearer still if you try a few smart playlist experiments of your own.

You can create playlists manually or you can create a smart playlist which automatically finds tracks by a particular composer, for example.

Author insight

If you like music while you work, create a playlist of your favourite 'ambient' music and set iTunes to 'loop' the playlist so that it starts again from the beginning when it's finished. (There's nothing more disruptive than having to stop work to choose some more music.)

10.5 Enjoying your music

iTunes can be used to play music directly on your Mac, though it's likely that the built-in speakers won't provide the kind of hi-fi quality you're looking for.

The solution is straightforward, provided you have enough room on your desk and don't mind a few extra cables – get an accessory speaker set. These can be as simple as the inexpensive stereo speakers you buy for PCs. These are powered by their own mains adaptor and plug into the Mac's earphone socket.

More expensive speaker sets will provide better quality, right up to the standard you might expect from a modest hi-fi system. These consist of two stereo speaker units as usual, plus a 'sub-woofer' for deeper, more powerful bass.

These aren't just useful for music. Many Mac users also use their computers to play back DVD movies, and a proper sound system will really enhance the experience, particularly if you have a Mac with one of the latest widescreen displays.

Whether you're using the Mac's built-in speakers or a sophisticated plug-in speaker system, it's possible to fine-tune the sound to match the capabilities of the speakers, the style of music you're listening to and your own preferences. iTunes has its own graphic equalizer, which you can display using the Window > Equalizer command.

Like other graphic equalizers, this one enables you to adjust the strength of a whole series of different frequency bands. That's fine for hi-fi nuts and audio technicians, but perhaps a little daunting for the rest of us. But there is an easier solution – the Equalizer window also has a pop-up menu with preset adjustments for different speaker types and music styles. For example, if you're playing music using the built-in speakers in MacBooks, the Small Speakers setting is likely to give the best results. When you're experimenting with the different settings, do allow a few seconds for them to take effect – the changes aren't instantaneous, and this can fool you into thinking nothing has happened.

To get better playback quality, try tweaking the iTunes Equalizer. For the best sound, though, you really need a good set of external speakers.

Author insight

It's worth investing in a good set of headphones. The Apple 'buds' you get with an iPod are OK, but not brilliant. If you use your iPod in noisy environments, you could try Sennheiser headphones, for example. They're a little more expensive, but they muffle out ambient noise and provide a much stronger bass effect.

iTunes has one more trick for those moods when you just want to chill out and lose yourself in the music. If you use the Window menu and Visualizer command, the iTunes window is taken over by randomly-generated patterns – although they're not truly random, since they respond to the music. The iTunes Visualizer might sound like a somewhat frivolous add-on, but actually it's quite fascinating to watch and can really draw you into the mood of the music.

You can also get the Visualizer to use the full screen.

1 Open the **iTunes** menus and choose **Preferences**, then click the **Advanced** tab of the Preferences dialog.

2 At the bottom is the **Display visualizer full screen** option. Tick this.

The Visualizer can also be activated using the [**Command**]-[**T**] shortcut. This also switches back to iTunes when you've had enough of watching those swirling patterns.

The iTunes Visualizer takes over your screen with patterns of light and colour which change in response to the music.

10.6 Creating audio CDs

One of the great things about iTunes is how easy it is to create audio CDs from tracks stored in your library.

Why would you want to do this, especially if you've just gone to the trouble of copying CDs to your library?

Well, CDs do have advantages. We mentioned one earlier – you might want to create some CDs to play back in your car stereo, or in a regular CD player. CDs are also a good way to back up any music you buy from the iTunes store, because until you do, they'll only exist as a digital file on your computer.

And one great advantage that your own CDs will have over the originals is that you can choose which tracks they contain, and the order they play in. After all, even our favourite artists can produce duds, and it's rare that we enjoy every single track on an album. In addition, with iTunes you can create your own 'best of' compilations using tracks from several different albums.

1 First, create a playlist containing the tracks you want to copy to the audio CD.

2 How do you know they will fit? Look at the bottom of the iTunes window when the playlist is selected. It will display the number of tracks (songs) and the total time. Depending on the CD type, 1 hour is around the maximum.

3 With the playlist still selected (you should see its tracks in the main window), click the **Burn Disc** button in the bottom right-hand corner of the iTunes window.

4 A message in the status panel at the top flashes, saying 'Please insert a blank disc...' Slide a blank

CD into the Mac's CD/DVD drive. The display will now say 'Checking disc...' Then the burning process begins – iTunes writes the tracks to the CD. This will just take a minute or so and, at the end of the process, iTunes has generated an audio CD which is now ready to play in any regular CD player.

And that really is all there is to it.

10.7 Synchronizing with iPods

One of the key points about iTunes is that you don't need an iPod to make good use of it. You can use it to copy and enjoy your CD collection, download music from the iTunes Store and create your own compilation CDs, as we've seen.

However, for those who want to enjoy their music on the move, an iPod is the obvious choice, simply because it integrates so perfectly with iTunes.

Other portable music players do exist, of course, but it may not be so easy to transfer your music to these. By default, iTunes uses the AAC format for music files, which is not the same as the MP3 format used by most other devices.

iTunes can be configured, however, to copy music in the MP3 format instead. This is done using the iTunes Preferences and the General tab. Here, you click the button for the Importing Settings, where there's a pop-up menu for changing the file format used. (In older versions, this can be found in the Advanced tab.)

Many third-party music players are compatible with iTunes, and will appear in the iTunes window as a device to which you can copy music. However, music downloaded from the iTunes store will only play on iPods and iTunes-compatible devices, which currently include certain mobile phones and, of course, the iPhone and iPad.

Needless to say, using an iPod with iTunes is simple. When you connect the iPod, its icon will appear in iTunes, which will do one of two things, depending on how it's been set up: iTunes will automatically synchronize your Library with the iPod (the default), or you can opt to manage your music manually.

Automatic synchronization is the simplest choice because it takes care of all the file transfers for you. If you create a new playlist, copy a new CD or buy new tracks from the iTunes store, they're automatically copied to the iPod the next time you connect it. But this only works if the capacity of the iPod is large enough for your entire music library. It won't be a problem with the iPod classic and larger-capacity iPod Touch models, nor with the iPhone and the iPad. With iPod Nanos, it's quite likely that your music library will soon be too large to fit. This is when you need to swap to the manual mode. To do this, you click the iPod's icon to display its Summary screen, and choose the appropriate options at the bottom.

Incidentally, you might want to explore the other sections of this window, because you can also synchronize podcasts, photos and even contacts from your Address Book to your iPod. If you connect an iPod Touch, iPhone or iPad, the sections will increase to include any downloaded apps.

When you manage music manually, you transfer tracks to the iPod by first selecting the Music button in the Library section, top left. Now you can select tracks from the main window and drag them on to the iPod icon, or drag Playlist icons on to it.

On the iPod, music is automatically sorted by artist, track and album name, so you can find the tracks you need that way – or, you can choose a playlist instead. Playlists are probably the best choice because it's not possible to change track orders on iPods – you can't program in your favourite tracks in the same way that you can in iTunes. Think of them simply as playback devices for music you've already organized in iTunes.

iTunes and iPods are designed to be used together so it's no surprise to learn that transferring songs and even synchronizing your music library is easy.

Author insight

If you've got an iPod, get an iPod docking station. You can play your music and charge your iPod at the same time, and without having to start up your Mac. Prices vary, but the more you pay the better the sound. It won't be as good as hi-fi separates, but the convenience of having an entire music collection at your fingertips makes up for it.

10.8 The iTunes store

Most readers will have noticed a trend away from conventional CDs towards music downloads. It's hard to predict right now whether this will ultimately spell the end of CDs, but that seems unlikely in the short term. Many consumers remain mistrustful of digital distribution and prefer the ownership of a real object (a CD) to a collection of digital files. However, music downloads do have many advantages, and for customers as well as distributors. For example, you can click the iTunes Store button in iTunes to access the iTunes Store via the Internet and search for specific tracks or albums which may be difficult to find in retail stores.

Now remember our remark earlier that you seldom enjoy all the tracks on an album? When you shop at the iTunes store, you can buy tracks individually (currently 99p in the UK), and this can work out cheaper for albums which contain just two or three classics (why pay for a whole bunch of others you don't really like?). Alternatively, you can buy the whole album – the price is listed, and it's easy enough to do the sums.

When you make a purchase, you don't get a CD sent to your house. It's not like buying from Amazon! Instead, the music is downloaded to your Mac when you make the transaction. These files are stored in your iTunes Library alongside your others. The album art (the cover) will also be downloaded and stored in iTunes to be displayed alongside the music you've bought.

It's a good idea at this point to burn a CD of your new purchase, just in case something happens to your Mac and you don't have any backups.

To buy from the iTunes Store you must set up an account, and this is where some buyers may be reluctant to proceed, as it means lodging your credit card details so that future transactions can be charged to your card automatically, although the Store will alert you to this and check that you want to proceed.

This will be a stumbling block for those who prefer transactions to be clear-cut, single payments. On the other hand, if you're prepared to accept the terms, costs and frequent uncertainties of a mobile phone contract, the iTunes Store is hardly any different. Indeed, it's far less likely you'll incur unexpected costs here. This is a payment method we may all have to get used to in the future as more and more companies seek to automate their payment services.

You can buy music from the iTunes store an album at a time or a song at a time, and it can all be done within the iTunes window.

Author insight

Try to get into the habit of rating your music in iTunes. You can then select the My Top Rated smart playlist to see (and play) all your favourite tracks in one place.

10.9 What's DRM?

Until recently the iTunes Store used DRM, or Digital Rights Management. This is the music industry's attempt to protect music from unauthorized copying, which is perceived as a much greater problem now that music can be downloaded.

Apple's DRM involved restrictions on the way downloaded music could be used. These were not imposed by Apple, but are requirements of the industry as a whole. These also applied with rival music download services – not just Apple. Downloaded music could only be played on up to five computers, synced with your iPod, synced or streamed to the Apple TV device or burned on to a CD. But Apple also offered tracks in a slightly more expensive 'iTunes Plus' format which had no usage limitation. This has now become the standard format for downloaded music, so although downloads are now slightly more expensive (99p rather than 79p), the whole situation is much simpler.

10.10 What are podcasts?

A Podcast is like a radio or a TV show you can download and play back via iTunes. Most are free, but some have to be paid for.

To see how it works, go to the iTunes Store (you don't need an account for this) and go to the Podcasts section, where you can browse sections devoted to comedy, sport, the arts, news and music. Podcasts are classified as video or audio and are illustrated

Podcasts are video or audio 'programmes', often free, which can be downloaded to iTunes individually or subscribed to as a series.

with small images and brief descriptions. To find out more, you click on the image.

Here you'll find that most podcasts come in several instalments, or episodes, which are shown as a list. This list will also tell you whether they are free or not. You can download individual episodes, or subscribe to the podcast so that new episodes are downloaded to iTunes automatically.

Podcasts are submitted to the iTunes Store by many publishers, and the list of available podcasts is already so long that you could spend an awful lot of time just browsing through them.

10.11 What's Internet radio?

But podcasts aren't the only way to enjoy broadcasts with iTunes. For those brought up on radio rather than television, iTunes and the Internet breathe new life into this unique medium.

It's all done with Internet radio, which has been made much more practical by high-speed broadband communications. First, click Radio in the iTunes Library section. iTunes will now list a whole range of music genres, including jazz or reggae, for example. Each of these expands into a whole list of Internet radio stations. To try one, double-click its name. In a few moments, you'll be connected to the radio station's live audio stream.

Internet radio isn't limited by transmitters, aerials and reception. As a result, you can listen to radio stations all over the world, from Belgrade to Boston, without interference or atmospherics. (Internet radio isn't unique to iTunes – it's built into Windows Media Player on PCs, too.)

Music and video downloads tend to grab all the headlines these days and Internet radio is often overlooked. And that's a shame, because there are some great radio stations out there which provide constantly-changing background music and even introduce you to new artists and genres you might never have encountered if you'd stuck to the same old predictable favourites you know already.

It's not been possible in this chapter to fully explore everything that iTunes can do or examine in great depth those things we have covered. Hopefully, though, you now know enough to start exploring this exciting new world of digital entertainment on your own.

Who said radio is dead? Now you can listen to stations from around the world, and without a 40-foot mast in your garden.

TEST

1 *Originally, iTunes was designed to connect to iPods, but it's now the sychronization tool for two new mobile devices. What are they?*

2 *How do you enter the track names when you record (import) a CD?*

3 *iTunes can display album covers, but where does it get them from?*

4 *What's the difference between a playlist and a smart playlist?*

5 *What are the Equalizer and the Visualizer?*

6 *When you're creating an audio CD, how do you know that the tracks you've chosen will fit?*

7 *iTunes can synchronize the contents of its entire music library with your iPod automatically, but when might that be a bad idea?*

8 *How much does the average song cost on the iTunes store?*

9 *Where can you find podcasts?*

10 *What is Internet Radio, and how does it differ from audio radio?*

11

iMovie and iDVD

In this chapter you will learn:
- *how to import video into iMovie*
- *how to organize and browse clips*
- *how to create projects*
- *how to add transitions, titles and voiceovers*
- *how to export finished movies*
- *how to create new iDVD projects*
- *where to find movie files*
- *how to change menu and title text*
- *what the Drop Zone is for*
- *how to burn a DVD*

11.1 What iMovie does

iMovie and iDVD are both involved in the creation of movies, and it can be difficult to understand where one leaves off and the other takes over.

In this chapter, then, we'll try to explain the difference simply and get you started with both programs so that you've got a clearer idea which you need, when and why.

There's a lot more to both programs than we cover here. Our aim is not to provide a complete reference, but to explain the basic concepts so that you can understand what you're able to do and you know broadly how to do it. All the step-by-step details can be found in the online Help.

We'll start with iMovie. iMovie is to movie clips what iPhoto is to still photographs. You use iMovie to import and organize all your video clips, whether they were shot on a camcorder or a digital camera.

iMovie goes further. With digital photos you can compose shots carefully to leave out unwanted detail. It's not so easy with video clips. Unexpected things happen. The action you're waiting for may take too long to arrive. Many of your video clips will include long sections where nothing much is happening. That's why videos need editing before they're fit for showing to other people, and that's the other thing that iMovie does. You can edit your clips and combine them in Projects which can then be exported as polished, standalone movies.

Use iMovie to import and organize your video clips.

The latest version is iMovie 09. This does include some enhancements over iMovie 08. These are mainly designed to make movies look better and easier to create, but the basic workings of the program are the same. The new features are:

► *Advanced drag and drop editing for quicker and easier movie-making*

- ▶ A *Precision Editor for finer control over the movie-making process*
- ▶ *Dynamic Themes (titles, transitions, etc.) for producing polished movies with little or no effort*
- ▶ *Animated travel maps*
- ▶ *Video stabilization to try to counter the effect of camera movement and shaky clips*
- ▶ *New titles, transitions and effects*
- ▶ *A full-screen library browser.*

Author insight

You can use digital photos as they are most of the time, but digital video always needs editing. This can be a time-consuming and technical process, but iMovie makes it easier than most video buffs would have thought possible.

11.2 What iDVD does

iDVD enables you to create DVDs with menus using your own movie clips.

The movies you create in iMovie can be played back on the Mac, uploaded to YouTube or emailed (if they're short enough) to your friends and relatives. But what if you want to create a movie on a DVD, one that will play back on a domestic DVD player?

Creating DVD movies, complete with titles and menus, requires special software – and that's what you need iDVD for. Although it might appear that iDVD and iMovie do a similar job – adding titles, combining movie clips – they're actually very different. iMovie is for combining clips into single movie files. iDVD is for converting one or more movie files into a DVD.

11.3 Getting clips into iMovie

First, we'll look at how to get movie clips into iMovie. These days there are a number of devices which can record video, including mobile phones. Here, though, we'll stick to the most common: MiniDV camcorders, solid state (hard disk or flash memory) camcorders and digital cameras.

The procedure for importing video from a digital camcorder will depend on whether it's an older tab-based device or a newer solid state model.

To import video from a tape-based MiniDV camcorder:

1 Rewind the tape to where you want to start recording and connect it to the Mac using a Firewire cable (you may need to get this separately).
2 Look for the Open Camera Import Window button in the iMovie window (it's the button with a camcorder icon).

To import video from a solid-state camcorder:

1 Connect the camera in the same way (it may use Firewire or USB).
2 If iMovie doesn't prompt you to import the movie(s) automatically, use the File > Import from Camera command.

3 In the Import window, choose the camcorder from the pop-up menu in the bottom left-hand corner (if you have a MacBook or an iMac, this will also list the built-in iSight camera).

4 Press the Capture button to start recording the camcorder footage.

5 iMovie will ask you where you want to store it – the Movies folder is the most logical place. You'll also be asked whether you want to store it in an existing project or a new one. Projects are explained in section 11.5.

If your video's been shot on a digital camera or some other solid state storage device, it may have been saved as separate video files. To import these, open the File menu and choose Import Movies. You can then browse the contents of your Mac to find the video clips you want to import.

What's especially clever is that iMovie will always break footage up into clips based on when the camera was stopped and started again.

Movie clips recorded on digital cameras can be copied to your hard disk and imported from there. Footage from camcorders can be imported by connecting the camcorder via its cable.

The import procedure will depend on the format the video is saved in, because it's not always a single file you can just copy across. This applies in particular to old-fashioned MiniDV tape camcorders and devices which shoot in the latest AVCHD format.

The sudden surge in HD movies does have an effect on how you shoot and edit movies now. HD movies take up more space, but they also demand more processing power for editing and playback. If you have an older or less powerful Mac, iMovie may warn you that the clips you're importing may not play back properly on your current hardware and offer an alternative, slightly lower resolution.

HD movies come in two resolutions: standard HD (1280 × 720 pixels) and full HD (1920 × 1080 pixels). Devices that just say 'HD' usually shoot at standard HD resolution.

Author insight

When you shoot a movie, think of it as a series of 'takes' rather than one, long sequence. It's better to think about what you want to film before you start, and shoot with a plan in mind, than it is to start the camera rolling and just follow the action around.

11.4 Organizing and browsing clips

The iMovie window has three main areas: the Event Library, the Project Library and the Preview panel.

The Event Library is like the events display in iPhoto. Instead of displaying movie clips individually, iMovie groups them into these events. You can click on an event to see all the movie clips it contains. You might set up an event to contain all the clips you shot on holiday, for example.

These clips aren't displayed as single thumbnail images (like they were in the previous version of iMovie, for example). Instead, they're displayed as filmstrips containing a series of thumbnails taken from the video at five-second intervals. Why do it this way?

It gives a clearer idea of the duration of a clip – longer clips produce longer filmstrips – and makes it easier to identify key points in the clip. If the five-second intervals produce too many thumbnails, use the slider in the bottom right-hand corner of the window to change the interval to ten seconds, say.

There's another slider in the top left-hand corner of the Event Library window. This is for changing the size of the thumbnails.

Now's the time to introduce iMovie's party trick. If you move the pointer over a clip, it plays back, and at the speed you're dragging the pointer. This makes it really easy to see what's happening in a clip and to skim to the points you want very quickly. As you move the mouse you'll see a vertical red bar moving across the clip. If you stop moving the mouse, this bar stops at that point in the clip. Now, if you press the spacebar, the movie plays at normal speed from that point – press the spacebar again to stop it.

Video clips are shown as a filmstrip and you can 'skim' through the footage simply by moving the mouse across it from left to right (or backwards from right to left).

11.5 Creating a project

As shot, movie clips tend to be rather raw. They need trimming and combining to produce a decent movie you'll be proud to show to others, and that's what the Project Library is for.

First, you use the '+' button at the bottom of the Project Library panel to create a project – you'll be prompted to choose between

4:3 and 16:9 aspect ratios. 4:3 is the ratio most camcorders and digital cameras shoot in by default; it's also that of traditional TV sets. Many camcorders and cameras can also shoot in the wider 16:9 ratio – the aspect ratio of today's widescreen TVs. Choose the ratio that matches the clips you'll use in the project.

Once the new project is created, you can drag clips on to it from the Event Library panel. Now this isn't quite as straightforward as simply dragging a thumbnail because moving the mouse pointer over a clip, as we saw earlier, plays back the clip. The alternative is to [Ctrl]-click the clip and choose Select Entire Clip from the menu. This places a yellow border around the whole clip and now you can drag it.

The Event Library is where you collect your raw video clips, but the Project Library is where you assemble them into movies.

But maybe you don't want the whole clip? Maybe you only want a part of it? In this case, move the red playback bar to the point in the clip where you want your selection to start and then drag until the end of the section you want. As you do this you'll see a yellow border pick out the section you've selected. You can now drag this selection to a project.

It's also possible to trim clips once they've been added to a project. Just select the section you want, open the Edit menu and choose Trim to Selection.

Once clips have been added to a project and you've trimmed them as necessary, you can rearrange them into the right order, ready for the next step...

....
Author insight

The key to good movies is shooting them right, not super-powerful software. Keep the camera still (ideally, on a tripod) and resist the urge to zoom in and out a dozen times during a single clip. It should be the subjects that are moving, not the camera.
....

11.6 Adding transitions

It's a bit unsubtle if one clip stops and another starts in the blink of an eye. Transitions are a standard movie technique for fading one scene into another. To add a transition between clips, click the Transitions Browser button in the bottom right-hand corner of the Project Library panel. A selection of pre-configured transitions appears in its own panel, and you can preview any of them by placing the mouse pointer over it. When you've found one you like, drag it from the Transitions panel and onto your project, positioning the mouse pointer carefully between the two clips you want to blend – they'll move apart slightly to make room for the transition.

To add a transition just choose it from this panel and drag it between two clips in your project.

11.7 Adding titles

It doesn't look quite right, either, if your movie just starts, without any kind of introduction. This is where you need a title screen and, again, you can add one using drag and drop. This time, click the Titles button in the bottom right corner of the Project Library. You'll see a selection of title layouts and, when you've found one you like drag it in front of the first clip in your project.

The Preview window will now show you the title screen and its dummy text. You need to type over this with your own text, and to do this, drag the mouse pointer over the text to select it and then type your own. And just to add that little finishing touch, why not add a transition between the title and the first clip?

Titles are added in the same way. This time, you choose the title you want and drag it in front of (or on to) the first clip before typing in your own text.

11.8 Adding a voiceover

Some of your clips will feature speech that hasn't come out too well, either because of wind noise or because the person speaking is too far away. Other clips desperately need some kind of commentary but don't have one. In both cases, the solution could be a voiceover added in iMovie. All you need is a Mac with a microphone.

1 Click the Voiceover button (the one with a picture of a microphone).

2 Do what the message on the screen tells you to do – click on the clip you want to add the voiceover to. You get a three-second countdown, and then the microphone starts recording as the playbar starts moving over the clip.

3 When you've said your piece, click the mouse to stop the recording.

Voiceovers don't replace any existing audio. Instead, the audio track that's already there is faded slightly and your voice commentary is added over it. When your commentary stops, the clip's audio is subtly faded back to its original volume.

This is what's so great about iMovie – it produces professional-looking results without any effort or know-how on your part. It does so much more, too, that we haven't been able to cover here, but which you'll enjoy discovering on your own now that you know how iMovie works.

Clips with poor or no sound may benefit from a voiceover. iMovie used the Mac's built-in microphone and subtly overlays the existing sound with your commentary.

Author insight

iMovie might be designed for beginners, but it can produce some very professional-looking movies, not least because of the new Precision Editor in iMovie 09. The main reason, though, is that it makes basic but essential techniques (clip editing, transitions, voiceovers, titles) simple enough for amateurs.

11.9 Exporting the movie

That's not quite the end, though. At the moment, the movie project can only be played back in iMovie. To send the finished project to other people you have to export it as a movie file. To do this, open the Share menu, where you'll see a whole host of options. For example you can send the movie to iTunes, where it can by synced to an iPod. You can send it to YouTube, if that's your thing, you can publish it to the Mac's Media Browser so that it's available for dragging and dropping into documents created by other applications like Pages and Keynote, and you can send it to a MobileMe Web Gallery if you have a MobileMe account.

If you want to create a DVD, though, you need to choose the Export Movie option. You'll be prompted to choose a name for the movie, the location where you want to save it and the output size (choose pixel dimensions close to those of the original recording device). iMovie will now export a movie file which you can import into iDVD...

11.10 Creating a new iDVD project

iDVD is a simpler program than iMovie because it only has one job – to turn regular movie files into DVDs with menus which can be played, like commercially-available DVDs, on domestic DVD players. (Actually, iDVD can also produce photo slideshows and mix them with videos, but we'll keep it simple for now.)

When you start iDVD, it will open the last project you worked on (if any) or prompt you to create a new one. iDVD, like other Mac software, offers ready-to-use templates to make the job as easy as possible. iDVD has a selection of themes which are displayed vertically down the right-hand side of the window. Each theme has different screens, titled Main, Chapters and Extras. To get started, just choose the Main screen from one of these themes.

iDVD comes with a range of very attractive-looking project templates to make your DVDs look really professional.

11.11 Importing video

This screen will now appear in the main window, ready for you to add your own content. To do this, click the Media button in the bottom right-hand corner of the iDVD window and then click the Movies button top right to show the contents of your iMovie Event Library and the Movies folder.

As you add movies to your project, iDVD adds them to the screen as a menu.

All you have to do now is drag a movie clip from the Media window on to the Main screen (but not on to the Drop Zone area). When you do this, a button will be added, labelled with the filename of the video file.

Now carry on adding as many video files as you want. iDVD will build a movie menu on the screen.

Author insight

If you want to shoot still photos and movies equally, get an up-to-date stills camera with an HD movie mode. If you want to shoot movies primarily and just grab a still now and again, get a camcorder. Still cameras are better at shooting movies than movie cameras are at shooting stills.

11.12 Simple modifications

At the moment, the movies are labelled with their filenames, which isn't very helpful. To change this to something more meaningful, click the text to select it and then again to make it editable. You can now type in a title of your own. You'll also notice that buttons appear directly below which let you change the font used and the size of the text.

That's not all you can do. We mentioned in the previous section that you shouldn't drop movies on to the Drop Zone area. This Drop Zone is for photos or movies which you want to play on the main screen while viewers are deciding which video clip to click on. You should choose something decorative or diverting rather than a clip which people need to pay attention to.

There's a lot more you can do with iDVD that's not covered here. The intention, though has been simply to get the basic principle across. The rest can be explored at your leisure – the online Help is very good, and there's a Getting Started PDF which you can print out and keep by your side as you experiment further with the features.

You can change the menu titles, and you can add photos or video clips to the 'Drop Zone' to personalize the menu page.

11.13 Burning a DVD

The final step in the process is to burn your DVD, and this option can be found on the File menu. iDVD is very helpful. It will check your project before it burns it and report any errors that you might want to attend to. You can also open a DVD map to check the structure of more complex DVDs, and use the Project Info dialog (from the Project menu) to check the space used and other technical information prior to burning the DVD.

TEST

1 *iMovie creates movies from video clips, but what is iDVD for?*

2 *What are the two main ways of importing video clips into iMovie?*

3 *HD movies are taking over, but there are two standards for resolution. What are they?*

4 *When you import clips into iMovie, where are they stored?*

5 *What do you need to do to turn the clips you've imported into a movie?*

6 *How do you preview a clip?*

7 *How do you blend one clip smoothly with another?*

8 *What are 'titles'?*

9 *What do you need to add a voiceover?*

10 *Can you share your movies online?*

Organize your life with iCal

In this chapter you will learn:
- *what iCal can do*
- *about the different calendars*
- *how to add an appointment or a To Do*
- *ways to remind yourself of upcoming events*
- *how to add a contact to your Address Book*
- *how to set up an email group*
- *about Smart Groups*

12.1 What does iCal do?

iCal is a digital diary. You can use it to keep track of all your appointments, jobs, meetings and social events. It comes as standard with all Macs, and you'll find its icon on the Dock.

iCal is laid out like a calendar, and there are buttons at the top to let you switch between Day, Week and Month views. Either side of these buttons are arrows for going backwards and forwards in time. iCal has a Sidebar, just like other Apple applications. This one has a list of calendars. Calendars are used to organize your appointments into work and personal items, for example, or to hep you manage different projects.

Depending on how iCal was set up when it was last used, there may be other items on the screen. In the bottom left-hand corner are three buttons: Add a New Calendar, View or Hide Mini-Month and View or Hide Notifications. These open a small panel in the bottom left which displays additional information.

Notifications are used when working alongside other iCal users, to request and organize meetings. The Mini-Month display can be useful for moving forward or backwards weeks or months at a time. We'll look at calendars shortly.

In the bottom right-hand corner of the window is a thumb tack button. This is used to show or hide your To Do list. When the To Do list is displayed, the main calendar display shrinks slightly to make room for it.

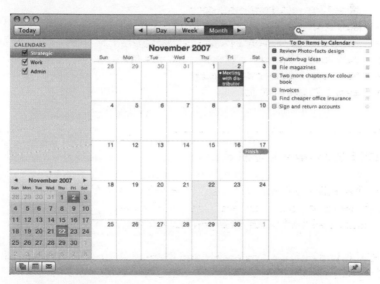

iCal acts as a digital diary, with day, week or month views and can also keep track of your To Do list.

Author insight

Not everyone will get on with a 'digital' organizer like iCal. It's all about balancing your own requirements against the tools available. iCal is clever, but if it doesn't suit you and you'd rather use pen and paper, that doesn't make you some kind of outdated reactionary. Don't let clever software make your needs look more complicated than they really are.

12.2 Creating an appointment

1 Use the buttons to move to the day you want to create it on (click the Today button to go straight to the current date).

2 Drag out an appointment over the time slot. You'll see a new event appear as you drag. When you release the mouse button, the 'New Event' text is highlighted ready for you to type in a title.

3 You can move this event, and alter its duration. To move it to a different time slot, or day, just drag the event. To change its start time or end time, move the pointer over the top or bottom edge and drag up or down.

12.3 Setting a reminder

How many times do you jot down an appointment and then forget all about it? With iCal you can set up reminders to give your memory a jog ahead of time.

1 Double-click the event you want to be reminded about.
2 This opens a window where you can change its properties – we're interested in the alarm setting roughly half-way down.
3 By default, the alarm is set to None, but if you click the pop-up menu you'll see there are other options. The most useful are Message and Email. If you choose Message, iCal will display a reminder in a dialog on the screen. If you choose Email, iCal will send you a reminder by email.
4 In both cases you can choose how many minutes, hours or days ahead of the event you get the reminder – you can also

choose a specific date for the reminder. If you select an email reminder, you can specify the address the reminder is sent to (this is useful if you have more than one email address, and perhaps one that you use when you're away from the office, for example).

The event dialog also lets you change the date(s) for the event – this is useful if you want to move it to a date outside the current view. You can set it to be an all-day event instead of occurring at a specific time, and you can also choose the calendar the event belongs to. We'll look at calendars next.

Worried you might forget what you've got to do? iCal can display an alert on the screen or send you an email reminder.

Author insight

If you set up a reminder for an upcoming event, an email reminder could be the best choice. After all, what if you're away from home and having to use a different computer. As long as you can check your emails online, you'll still get your reminder.

12.4 Using multiple calendars

Do you keep one diary for work and one for home? In iCal you can separate these different aspects of your life by using different calendars within iCal. You can create as many as you like. To start with, you might find just a single calendar is all you need – it's certainly the least confusing setup to begin with.

Calendars, as we saw earlier, are listed in the Sidebar to the left of the iCal window.

1 To create a new calendar, use the button at the bottom left of the window.
2 To change a calendar's name, just double-click it and type in the new name.
3 To change a calendar's colour-coding, select it and use the [Command]-[I] shortcut to open its info panel. The colour pop-up is in the top right-hand corner.

Each event you create is assigned to one of these calendars, and it shows up in that calendar's colour. These calendars do more than provide a quick colour-coding system, though. Do you see the checkboxes to the left of the calendar names? To hide a calendar, uncheck its box. To show it again, recheck the box. In this way, you can choose exactly which events are displayed, and this can make it easier to plan and schedule.

If you only want to see one calendar out of several, it's a bit laborious deselecting them all one-by-one, but there is a quicker way. Hold down [Command] as you click on any calendar's checkbox – this will hide them all. Now you just click the box for the calendar you want to see.

Author insight

If you have a MobileMe account you can store your calendar online in 'the cloud'. But you could also go the third-party route and use a free service like Google Calendar. It's entirely online and accessed via your web browser, so you can check your appointments on any computer with an Internet connection.

These colour-coded calendars look very pretty and do allow a lot of flexibility, but it's easy to get seduced by the novelty and set up lots of calendars you don't really need. You may find that you waste too much time assigning events to the correct calendars, and that a single calendar is both simpler and a lot quicker to work with.

12.5 Adding a To Do

As well as handling events, iCal can track all those jobs you know you've got to do at some point, but which don't require specific time slots. Like renewing your car insurance, for example, or organizing tickets for a business trip.

To create a To Do:

1 Display the To Do list using the button in the bottom right-hand corner of the iCal window.
2 A new To Do appears with its title already highlighted ready for you to type in your own. Note that new To Dos are always assigned to the currently selected calendar. If you select the calendar before you create a To Do (or an event, for that matter), it saves having to choose the calendar later.
3 New To Dos created in this way don't have a specific completion date. They stay on your list of To Dos for ever until they're done – when they are, click the checkbox to the left of the To Do. This indicates to iCal that the job's been done and it disappears from the list.
4 To set a deadline (completion date) for a To Do, double-click it to open its info window. Here, you check the Due date box, whereupon the palette produces a date display where you can enter the date you want and, below that, is an option to send yourself a reminder (alarm) – these work like event reminders.

You'll see from this window that you can also set a Priority of Low, Medium or High. This can be useful if your To Do list is very long and you're self-disciplined enough to approach it in a systematic,

methodical fashion. At the top of the To Do list is a To Do
Items pop-up which lets you sort your To Dos by Due Date
or Priority.

You might decide the only way to get a To Do done is to assign it
a time slot. To do this, just drag a To Do onto the calendar display
to create a new event, adjusting its duration, start time and date
as necessary. Similarly, you might decide that you need to prepare
items or carry out certain tasks in advance of a forthcoming event.
In which case, drag the event on to the To Do list, and choose
a suitable title and due date for the new To Do.

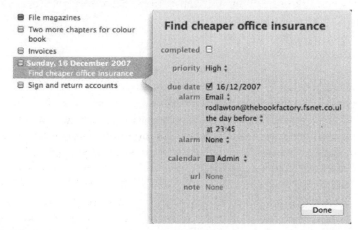

To Dos can simply be left floating, or they can be given a specific completion date, a priority and an alarm so that you don't forget them!

12.6 Viewing your To Dos in Mail

One of the new features in Mail is the ability to enter To Dos. These
are the same To Dos you see in iCal, even though the screen layout
is different. When you create a new To Do in iCal, it appears in
Mail, and vice versa.

This brings the Mac into line with Entourage, the personal
information manager and email program supplied with the Mac

version of Microsoft Office, and with Microsoft Outlook on the PC. People want their calendars, address books and email all linked together, and that's what the Mac now does.

To Dos you create in iCal appear in Mail, and vice versa.

Author insight

Apple Mail displays the same tasks that you see in iCal, but (in your author's opinion at least), it's a rather messy and unconvincing implementation. Also, for many people, tasks and events are different varieties of the same thing, whereas iCal treats them as separate.

12.7 What does Address Book do?

iCal takes care of events and To Dos, Mail takes care of your email messages (and To Dos) and both link to Address Book, the third in the Mac's trio of personal information management tools.

At a basic level, Address Book is simply a repository for all the email addresses you need in Mail. When you receive an email message you can click the sender's name to display a pop-up menu with the option to save their details to your Address Book. To send an email, you enter the recipient's name or nickname in the To: field and Mail will use the Address Book to look up their full email address.

Address Book can also be opened and used on its own – you'll find its icon on the Dock. The window has three vertical panels for groups, names and contact details respectively.

Let's say you want to add a phone number or an address for one of your contacts.

1 Type their name into the search box, top right – this is the quickest way to find people once your list goes beyond a couple of dozen entries.
2 Address Book will list all the matching names – select the one you want, to display the contact information to the right.
3 Click the **Edit** button at the bottom. It's now possible to modify and add contact information.
4 When you've finished, click the **Edit** button again.

Address Book isn't just an accessory for the Mail program, then, but a useful standalone program for looking up phone numbers, street addresses and even notes about individuals. This can prove useful at work for jotting down information about business contacts, and at home when you're building a list of things to get your partner for his or her birthday!

You'll note that Address Book can store multiple phone numbers, including mobile and fax numbers, and even the names of friends

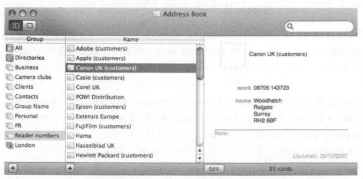

Address Book isn't just for email addresses. You can use it to store phone numbers, postal addresses and more.

or assistants. See the green '+' and red '–' buttons? You can use these to add or remove phone numbers or email addresses, and use the pop-up menus alongside to indicate whether they're for work or home.

> ## Author insight
> It's always worth adding new people to the Address Book as a matter or habit, because you never know when you might need to get in touch again. This is especially true in business, where old contacts often turn up in new roles many years later!

12.8 Organizing contacts into groups

But what about these groups? Well, sometimes you want to send the same message to lots of different people at once. It may be necessary to send out a regular bulletin to members of your team at work, or you may be the secretary of a club or society, with the job of keeping members up to date on what's happening.

1 Create a new group using the '+' button in the bottom left-hand corner and give it a name.
2 You can add people to this group by first clicking **All** at the top of the **Group** column and either scrolling through the list of contacts on the right or using the search box to find specific individuals.
3 When you've found a contact who needs to be added to the group, drag them from the **Name** column onto that group.

Now groups can be useful within Address Book for narrowing down the list of people to those related to work, home or other areas of your life. But they come into their own when you need to send bulk emails.

To do this, instead of typing the name of an individual into the message's To: field, open Address Book so that its window is in front of the Mail window, then drag a group into the To: field.

This is a very powerful feature, so make sure you really do want to send the message to all these people!

12.9 Smart Groups

iPhoto has smart albums, the Finder has smart folders, and Address Book has smart groups. It's a new feature which could be easily overlooked by those who don't know it's there.

Like the Smart tools in other Apple programs, smart groups display contacts whose details match certain specific criteria that you specify.

As an example, let's say we want a group that contains all our contacts who live or work in London. We know that this is indicated by telephone numbers that begin with '0207' or '0208', so this can be our smart group criterion. (We could also do this based on postcodes, but while we have landline telephone numbers for all these people, we don't have all their addresses.)

1 Choose **New Smart Group** from the **File** menu and give a name to the group – we're calling ours London.

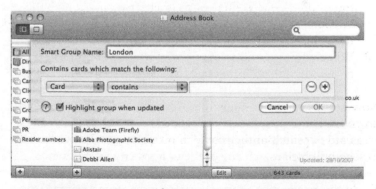

2 Now choose the criteria for the group. We set the first pop-up to **Phone** because it's phone numbers we're looking for.

The next pop-up is set to begins with and in the third box we type '0207' as the London area code.

3 Some London numbers start with '0208', though, so we need to click the '+' button to the right of the first criterion to add another one. For this second criterion, we repeat the steps we took for the first, but this time type '0208' in the box.

4 Now these Smart tools can work in two ways. They can be used to search for items which match all the criteria, or for items which match any of them. It's a crucial difference. In this case, we're looking for 0207 or 0208 numbers, so we need to set the pop-up above the search criteria to **Any** rather than **All**.

There's much more to Address Book and the way it can be used with other Mac applications than we've had the space to explain here, but hopefully we've helped you get started at least. Between them iCal, Mail and Address book can really help you get your life organized. But if you find it all too much fuss, don't despair. Some of us still get on much better using nothing more sophisticated than a pen and paper. Just because your Mac can do all these things, it doesn't mean you have to go along with it. Computers are there to assist our way of working, not define it!

TEST

1 *How do you display a To Do list alongside your calendar?*

2 *How do you move an appointment or change its duration?*

3 *How does iCal send you reminders of upcoming appointments?*

4 *Why would you use multiple calendars?*

5 *You may decide that a To Do item needs to be converted into an appointment. How do you do this?*

6 *What other program displays your To Do list and why?*

7 *Address Book stores email addresses for Mail, but what else?*

8 *What are Address Groups?*

9 *What's one of the key advantages of using Groups?*

10 *What's different about Smart Groups?*

13

....

Get online with iWeb

In this chapter you will learn:
- *how to create your first website*
- *how to type in your own website content*
- *how to add objects to web pages*
- *how to create websites with multiple pages*
- *how to set up a blog*
- *how to get your website online*

13.1 Getting started

iWeb enables you to create attractive websites easily, using ready-made templates. This chapter uses screenshots from iWeb 08, but where there are changes in iWeb 09, they will be explained.

When it's started for the first time, iWeb prompts you to create a site and choose a template. After that, it opens to display this website and any others you create in the program window. This window consists of a main panel which displays the web page currently being worked on, while at the left is a Sidebar which lists all the websites you've created and the pages within them. Each web page is displayed as a heading with a 'globe' icon, and alongside it is a drop-down arrow which is used to 'expand' or 'collapse' the list of pages in the website.

It's possible to create many web pages within a website, or just to one, depending on what you want the website to do. To begin with, stick to a single page to get an idea of how iWeb works.

Author insight

Skilled designers won't have difficulty finding fault with iWeb. You can't edit the HTML code directly, for example, and you can't apply designs and styles globally across the whole site. That misses the point, though. iWeb enables users who've never attempted to create a website before to have a go and actually come up with something rather good.

1 Choose **New Site** from the **File** menu. This displays a dialog with a list of website templates on the left. You click on one of these templates to see a list of page designs on the right.

2 Let's say we choose the Night Life template and the About Me page design. iWeb now displays this page in the main window. You'll notice that it's also created a new site in the sidebar and an About Me page within that site.

3 Make sure the About Me page is selected. Whichever page is highlighted in the sidebar is displayed in the main window. What if you change your mind about the design? Click the pop-up **Theme** button underneath and choose a new design.

The great thing about iWeb is that it's a WYSIWYG editor (What You See Is What You Get) and you can simply drag objects around to put them where you like. Web designers will know that's not a straightforward thing to do normally, and that it requires some very complicated code. iWeb, however takes care of this automatically behind the scenes.

13.2 Adding your own text

iWeb's page templates look like finished pages, but the intention is, of course, that you replace what's there with your own information. (Most users find it less daunting to start with a finished page which they adapt rather than a blank sheet they have to fill from scratch.) Let's start by changing the name on the About Me page. To do this, click on it (you may have to click twice – once to select the box the text is in, and once to select the text). This is placeholder text – it's designed to be typed over, so a single click selects a line or paragraph at a time. It's the same with all the text on the page. To change it, select it and type. The templates and text boxes are flexible, so that if you type more text than was there before, other objects move to make space.

Sometimes, when you're typing text into a smaller box – a heading, for example – the text flows on to another line and overlaps objects below. To fix this, click outside the box to deselect the text, then click the box once to select it. Text boxes have handles on the corners and edges. You can drag these handles to change the size of the box, or drag the centre of the box to change its position on the page.

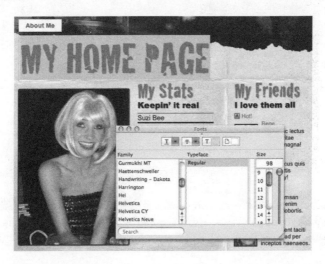

To change the text's size, colour or font, click the Fonts button in the bottom right-hand corner of the iWeb window. Unless you've got a particular reason to change them, though, it's best to leave the text styles alone because they've been carefully designed to tie in together as part of the overall design theme.

13.3 Adding your own photos

Most of the iWeb page templates contain photos and these, again, are 'placeholders' which simply show you what the finished page can look like. You can replace a photo in one of two ways:

1 If you know where it's stored on your Mac's hard disk, open a **Finder** window, locate the photo and simply drag its icon onto the existing placeholder photo on the web page. The picture will be scaled to fit the space automatically.

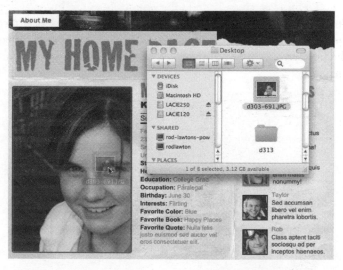

2 Click the **Media** button on the toolbar at the bottom of the iWeb window. This opens a palette showing the contents of your iPhoto library (see how well these Apple programs work

together?). You can use this to find the photo you want and drag it onto the web page.

Here, iWeb 09 is slightly different. The Media panel is now fixed to the side of the iWeb window instead of floating over it. There's also a new panel called 'Widgets', which is explained at the end of this chapter.

Author insight

If you want to put a collection of photos in iPhoto online, and you don't have a MobileMe account, you can send them to iWeb instead (there's a button on the toolbar) and create a photo gallery which you can upload to another web hosting company using the FTP support now built into iWeb 09.

13.4 Adding other objects

It's possible to do much more than just modifying objects that are already on the web page. You can delete existing template items, move them around and insert extra objects of your own.

To delete an object, click on it once to select it and hit [**Backspace**].

To duplicate an object (let's say you want another text box), select it and use the [**Command**]-[**D**] shortcut.

To create a new text box, click the Text Box button on the toolbar. iWeb creates a new, empty text box – it's not always obvious on some of the busier web page designs, so look closely.

To add a photo, open a Finder window or the Media palette as before, and drag it on to the web page. You can change the size of the photo by dragging its handles.

You can have a lot of fun experimenting with iWeb's different themes, customizing the text and graphics and adding your own web page content.

As you work with objects on web pages, you'll notice horizontal or vertical blue lines flashing up on the screen now and again. These are smart guides which help you align objects with others by showing you where the centres and edges are and 'snapping' objects into alignment. This helps the web page look better organized and more professional.

There's lots more to learn about text, photos and arranging web pages, but it's easy enough to pick that up as you go along with the assistance of the online Help. For now, we're going to concentrate on another important aspect of web design – building websites with more than one page.

Author insight

iWeb's strength is the fact that it works like a desktop publishing tool rather than a web editor. You can put text and pictures where they look right without having to worry about HTML code, CSS and everything else that makes web design such a complicated business.

13.5 Building a website

A website with a single page may be enough for telling other people about yourself, but most people will want to set up extra pages to cover different topics. That's why there are several page layouts in iWeb for each design theme.

1 To add a page, choose **New Page** from the **File** menu. This displays the template window you saw when you first created the site. Note that you can mix pages from different design themes in your website. It's possible, but it's not recommended! It might be colourful, but it will also look rather crass and amateurish.

2 Let's say you've already got an About Me page. Maybe you want to start a blog (there's more on blogs in the next section). To do this, choose the Blog template.

3 The sidebar now displays the new page underneath the first under your site heading. (Actually, blogs are a special case because they have more than one page, but we'll come to that in a moment.)

4 Something else has happened. You may have noticed that the original page had a small **About Me** button in the top left-hand corner. Now, there are two buttons: **About Me** and **Blog**. When the website is published online, these buttons act as links to these pages so that you can easily jump from one page to another.

What iWeb is doing here is creating a navigation bar automatically. Every time a page is added to the site, it's also added to the navigation bar. This makes life a lot easier for you as you build the site, and for other people when they visit it.

There are other ways of linking the pages on your site – or of adding links to pages elsewhere on the Internet.

Author insight

If you're serious about setting up and running a website, you'll need a proper commercial 'web host'. MobileMe is all right, but the servers aren't terrible fast (your pages can be slow to load), and while it integrates perfectly with iWeb, iPhoto and other Mac applications, you'll probably want to use third-party web design tools.

The About Me page has a links section already, in the bottom right-hand corner. At the moment, these links are dead – they're examples only, and not connected to anything. Setting up a link, though, is easy:

1 Create and/or select the text which is to form the hyperlink. This can be the web address itself, or just the name of the site.

2 Open the Insert menu, choose **Hyperlink** then select **Webpage** from the sub-menu.

3 This displays the **Link Inspector,** where you type the URL
(Internet address) of the page you want to link to.

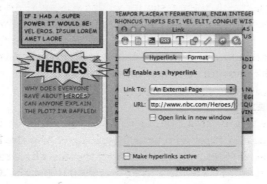

13.6 Websites versus blogs

Unless you've been living in a cave for the past few years, you'll be
aware that blogs are the Internet's Big Thing right now. You're no
one if you don't have a blog, and blogs – if we are to believe what
we hear – are proof of the democratic power of the Internet and
how the smallest individual now has as big a voice as the largest
multinational.

What few people actually attempt to do, though, is explain what
a blog actually is, so here goes…

Regular web pages are designed largely as static reference sources.
The pages are written and published and visited by people who
want to read them. Now and again, the information may need
updating, and the pages are then rewritten and republished. It's like
a book which is on the shelves for a certain amount of time then,
after a while, updated and republished as a new edition.

Blogs are different. Blogs are like diaries, or journals. The point of
a diary is not just what it says today, but what it said yesterday,
and the day before and so on. They're fascinating because they

give a glimpse back in time. It can add an extra dimension to an unfolding news story, or to your own opinions over time.

Many topical stories are revealed in a more interesting way by blogs. What's interesting is the way the facts, the journalist's own understanding and general public opinion change over time. Most news stories are two-dimensional, whether they're on a printed page or a website. In a blog, they become three-dimensional.

It's not just journalists who write blogs. If you help run a club, a blog is a much better way of keeping in touch with your members, partly because they can look up information in back issues of your blog and partly because adding new blog entries is easier than continually updating a regular website.

Blogs are simpler than websites in some ways and more complicated in others. They're simpler in that each new blog entry is generally just a single page which is written to a template and, with practice, can be produced quite quickly. But they're more complicated in another sense because each blog entry is moved to an archive when the next one is added. Visitors to the blog can not only read the current blog entry but search all the archived entries for information too.

That's why Blog pages in iWeb look more complicated in the sidebar. Each page has two sub-items: Entries and Archive.

The Entries page is where you do most of your work. This is split into a conventional web page display at the bottom and a list of entries at the top. To begin with, there's only one entry – the one you're working on. When you want to add another, click the Add Entry button beneath the list. The previous entry then becomes part of the Archive.

Here's a tip. If you use the Add Entry button, iWeb adds another template page and you'll have to type in your own headings and add your own pictures all over again. To avoid this, customize the blog page template once, and then duplicate this entry (press [**Command**]-[**D**]) to create a new one.

You can also click the Archive page in the sidebar to edit it in the main window. You don't see all your previous blog entries here because those are managed automatically online. Instead, you simply see the archive page furniture, and this is what you can modify.

Blogs in iWeb are much easier to understand once you start working on them. And for those with a MobileMe account, they're really simple to set up and maintain.

It's worth pointing out, though, that there are other, free blogging services which offer a bit more flexibility. Google's Blogger (www.blogger.com) is the easiest, but WordPress (www.wordpress.com) offers more tools and customization. These are great ways to start a blog, whether or not you have a MobileMe account.

With iWeb you can use a conventional web page as an introduction to one or more blogs. Blogs are like online journals and are both easier to maintain and more digestible for visitors than big websites.

13.7 Going live

There are now three ways of publishing your finished website. You can create many websites in iWeb, and each one will be listed in the sidebar. If you click on the site name (as opposed to any individual pages within it), you'll see the Site Publishing Settings. You can publish to MobileMe (if you have an account), to an FTP server (you will need to create an account with a web host, unless your Internet provider offers some free web space), or to a Local Folder.

FTP stands for File Transfer Protocol. It's a standard way of transferring files from one computer to another over the Internet. When you download an application or a software update, it's usually via FTP, though since this is normally handled automatically by the web browser, you're unlikely to notice.

When you publish a website online, it works the other way round. This time you're uploading files to a web server instead of downloading them. It's still done with FTP, though.

iWeb 09 now offers three ways to get your site online, including a new option to upload your site to an FTP server.

If you have a MobileMe account, this is the easiest option. The MobileMe account details will already have been set up, and iWeb now handles the upload process automatically.

When it's completed, iWeb will display the new web address for you. You can also visit published pages from within iWeb by first selecting the page in the sidebar and then clicking the Visit button below.

iWeb is set up to work seamlessly with a MobileMe account, as you might expect, and while many users in the UK might baulk at the prospect of having to pay an annual subscription when they're used to getting web services for nothing, in this case MobileMe is so useful – not just within iWeb – that it really is worth considering.

But if you don't have a MobileMe account, it's still possible to get your websites online by first publishing them to a Local Folder (a folder on your hard disk, in other words) and then uploading them separately using an FTP program:

1 In iWeb 08, instead of clicking the **Publish** button, click the site in the sidebar to select it, open the **File** menu and choose **Publish to a Folder**. You can now navigate to a folder or create a new one where all the files needed for the site will be saved. In iWeb 09, choose **Local Folder** in the **Site Settings** panel. You'll now be asked to choose the folder where you want to save your site.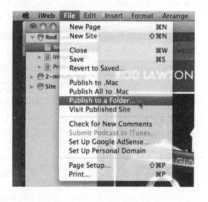

2 You'll need some online web space for storing your site – some Internet accounts come with free web space, so check with your provider. Otherwise, you'll need to shop around for a web hosting service. They will also be able to tell you the address to send your files to, and the username and password to use, together with any other relevant technical information. To upload the files, you'll need a program called an FTP client. There are free or trial versions available online, and while FTP clients can seem technical, they're usually pretty

straightforward once you've done it a couple of times. The one illustrated here is called CyberDuck.

The FTP publishing option introduced in iWeb 09 is a significant step forward, though. Previously, iWeb was rather churlish about letting you use any other web hosting service than MobileMe. Now, though, it's quite straightforward to choose another web host and enter the upload details into iWeb. In effect, iWeb is acting as your FTP program, so that you no longer need to export your site and upload it separately.

A web host is simply a company that offers online web space in exchange for a monthly fee. Few companies run their own web servers because it requires complex and expensive hardware and trained technicians. You can take a look at www.1and1.co.uk to get an idea of what web hosting companies offer.

Author insight

Did you know you can make money from your websites? You can do it through Google's Adsense scheme, which is supported directly by iWeb. Adsense scans your page to display a series of relevant ads, and each time a visitor clicks on an ad, you get a tiny fee. If your site's sufficiently popular, these fees could add up into a modest but potentially useful source of income.

13.8 Widgets

Widgets are a new feature in iWork 09, and they're a great way to add interesting and exciting content to your web pages without having to know anything about web design.

Actually, though, this isn't quite as new as it first appears. iWeb 08 allows you to add 'HTML snippets', and Widgets are actually little bits of code which you can cut and paste into these snippets.

What's different about iWeb 09 is the Media sidebar and the Widgets tab, and the fact that iWeb comes with a small selection as standard. You can add Google Maps, a Countdown Timer or an iSight Movie to your web page, for example. But the HTML Snippet widget is the one that offers the most

The Widgets panel is new in iWeb 09, but you can add widgets of your own with HTML Snippets, which were a feature of iWeb 08 too.

potential. With this you can simply paste in widgets from a variety of sources, like www.widgetbox.com.

An HTML Snippet is simply a little piece of code which operates in its own little window within the web page.

TEST

1   What does WYSIWYG stand for?

2   How do you add your own photos to a web page?

3   What are 'smart guides'?

4   What iWeb feature takes care of navigation automatically on multi-page websites?

5   What's different about blogs versus websites?

6   You can create blogs without iWeb, and there are two particularly well-known blogging services – what are they?

7   What does FTP stand for, and what is it?

8   What has been added in iWeb 09 to make publishing your site easier?

9   What is a 'web host'?

10 What are 'widgets', and what do they do?

14

....

MobileMe

In this chapter you will learn:
- *what the MobileMe service offers*
- *the pros and cons of MobileMe email*
- *how MobileMe can synchronize data between devices*
- *how MobileMe web galleries work*
- *about MobileMe's contacts and calendar*
- *how the iDisk is like a 10Gb virtual disk drive*
- *how MobileMe can help you find a lost iPhone*
- *what the iWork.com service offers and what makes it different*

14.1 What is MobileMe?

MobileMe is the new face of Apple's original .Mac service. It's a collection of online tools and features which work together to help you store and access your data online, share photos and more with others and synchronize calendars, emails and contact information between different devices.

This is especially important now, with snowballing popularity of iPhones and iPads. With MobileMe, the information you've stored on your desktop Mac can be synchronized automatically with your iPhone and your MacBook, and vice versa. Your data is the same on each device you own, and updated automatically wherever and however you type it in. You can also view your data online, using any web browser on any computer.

Note that this only applies to your emails, calendar entries and other organizer-style information. It doesn't apply to work files and things like that, though you can use the iDisk feature for that, and we'll also mention the iWork.com sharing site.

MobileMe is an extended set of online services available to Mac users for an annual subscription. The cost (£59 in the UK) might prove a sticking point for anyone accustomed to getting web services for nothing, but MobileMe is a little different from most free web tools.

- ▶ *First, it's not cluttered up with ads (these are what pay the bills for other providers).*
- ▶ *Second, it does things no other web services do.*
- ▶ *Third, it integrates seamlessly with the Mac OS and its applications in ways we're about to describe.*

And you can check these features out for yourself at www.apple.com/uk/mobileme, or by trying the 60-day free trial available at me.com (perhaps the world's shortest web address!).

MobileMe consists of a suite of six online tools for accessing and synchronizing key data on your Mac and mobile devices.

Author insight

There's nothing that MobileMe can do that you can't achieve, in a roundabout way, with various free online tools and services. But what you're paying for is simplicity and integration, not just features. Cycling is free, but sometimes it's just simpler to get a taxi.

14.2 Mail

MobileMe Mail is the online equivalent of the Mac's mail program, and it's the first of the MobileMe applications you see when you log into your MobileMe account.

Instead of downloading your mail to your Mac, it displays it online using Safari or any other web browser. This is an example of a web-based email system. Others include Google Mail (Gmail) and Yahoo Mail. You check your emails using a regular web browser rather than an email program.

The disadvantage is that your emails are stored online rather than on your computer, so you need to be online to read them. That's less of a problem these days than it might have been because most of us now use permanently-on broadband Internet access.

There are many advantages. The main one is that you can check your emails and reply to them using any web browser on any computer. This is perfect if you work on more than one computer or you need to access your mail while you're working away from home. All you need is your username and password.

MobileMe is also set up with Apple's Mobile devices in mind, particularly the iPhone. The name change from '.Mac' to 'MobileMe' might have seemed strange at the time, but it makes sense now that the iPhone has become so popular and the iPad has been launched. MobileMe can 'push' content between your devices, so that your emails and other data (Calendar and Contacts) are the same on all your devices.

It's up to you whether you use MobileMe to handle your emails on your Mac, or the Mail program on the Mac itself. There are differences in the way they look, and also in what they can do.

MobileMe Mail is designed to work with the email address you get with your MobileMe account. It can be used to check ordinary email accounts you already have, but it's easier and more effective to do this with the desktop Mail program and there are, besides, some complications which arise if you want to access other accounts too.

The main one is that MobileMe synchronization works solely with your MobileMe email account. You can access other accounts using MobileMe and the desktop Mail program, but the messages won't be synchronized.

One workaround is to forward messages to your MobileMe email account rather than fetching them directly, but this still brings complications for those who want their replies to appear to come from their other account rather than MobileMe.

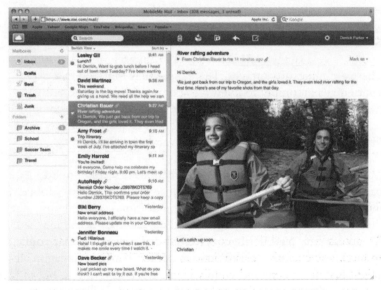

As long as you don't mind sticking to a single MobileMe email address for the sake of simplicity and full synchronization, MobileMe Mail is an excellent alternative to the desktop Mail program.

If all this is starting to sound complicated, that's because it is. MobileMe's Mail and synchronization features only work fully with MobileMe email accounts. This is not very well explained in Apple's documentation and could be a disappointment for those expecting a bit more.

But for those who don't mind sticking with their MobileMe email address, MobileMe Mail offers considerable advantages. It's also a very useful and attractive email tool. Unlike Gmail and other free web email services, it doesn't display ads alongside your message. You get a very clean interface laid out just like a regular desktop email program, with a list of folders in a vertical panel on the left and messages displayed in a dual-pane window on the right. One pane lists the message titles, and the other displays the contents of any message you click on.

You can set up as many folders ('Mailboxes') for storing your emails as you need, and message 'rules' for filing them automatically. And there's a very useful 'widescreen' view which displays these panes vertically alongside each other to make the most of the Mac's widescreen displays.

Author insight

If you've already collected a series of different email accounts that you need to keep track of (almost inevitable if you've been using computers for a while), then MobileMe Mail really just doesn't work very well. You're better off with Google Mail, which can access many different accounts online, and which you can access from any computer.

14.3 Contacts

To access your MobileMe contacts (and all the MobileMe tools, in fact), you click the 'cloud' icon in the top left-hand corner. This might just like a cute-and-cuddly icon chosen at random, but in fact it's a visual representation of 'cloud' computing, where you store your data online rather than on a single desktop computer.

The Contacts screen on MobileMe might look slightly different, but it displays the contents of your Mac's Address Book, and works in just the same way. The vertical sidebar on the left displays all the Address Book groups you've set up, and clicking on any of these displays an alphabetical list of contacts in another panel to the right. Clicking on any of these displays the contact's details in the main window.

This solves the problem of looking up phone numbers and addresses while you're away from your computer. Like all the other MobileMe apps, it can be accessed on any computer, Mac or PC, with an Internet connection.

MobileMe stores all your contacts online, synchronizing them with your Mac's Address Book automatically.

14.4 Calendar

The MobileMe Calendar synchronizes automatically with iCal on your Mac, so that both display the same calendars and the same appointments. You can make changes either on the Mac or on MobileMe, and they'll appear on both. This also applies to your iPhone or iPad, if you have one.

And because you can access your MobileMe calendar from any computer with an Internet connection, it's far more flexible than iCal if you often work away from your base. Again, it doesn't look quite like the iCal interface, but the calendars, events and tasks work in exactly the same way.

Although it works within a web browser, it works just like a desktop application. You can drag tasks on to the calendar display to create events and double-click on an event to edit its details.

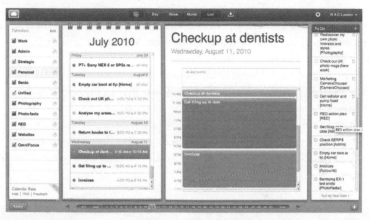

This is the MobileMe Calendar's List view. It displays your calendars on the left and a list of upcoming events alongside. The day's events are shown in the next panel and your tasks on the right.

14.5 Gallery

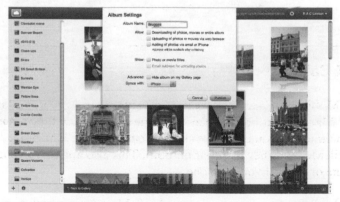

You can use the MobileMe Gallery section to check and modify any photo galleries you've set up in iPhoto.

Galleries are one of MobileMe's best features. When you create a MobileMe photo gallery in iPhoto, you're given an email address to send to other people so that they can visit your gallery.

The Gallery section in MobileMe lets you examine these albums, change the order of the pictures, change the titles and more. You can also change the access/uploading settings. Generally, you would choose all the settings when you create galleries in iPhoto, but you can check them and adjust them here if you need to.

It's worth having a MobileMe account almost for the photo galleries alone. It's really easy to set them up in iPhoto, and they synchronize automatically with your Mac, so that if you make an changes in iPhoto, the online photo gallery is updated. And if you set your galleries up so that you or others can upload photos to them online, these additions are synchronized with your iPhoto library.

MobileMe displays galleries using features and effects you don't get with ordinary photo gallery websites. Visitors view your galleries separately using a custom web address set up when the gallery is created.

14.6 iDisk

iDisk is the online storage component of your MobileMe account. It's like an online hard disk, and you currently get 20Gb of storage space split between Mail and general storage. When you have a MobileMe account, an iDisk icon appears in the Finder sidebar, and you can click on this and browse the contents just as you would your own hard disk (though it's a little slower).

The iDisk is where MobileMe stores your photo galleries, any websites you create in iWeb, and sundry other files. There's also a Public folder where you can share files with other people. They can use a web browser or a free Apple iDisk app to download them. This is useful for files which are too big to email. You can use other services like www.yousendit.com too, though file transfer sites generally have time limits, whereas with iDisk the files can be made available indefinitely.

Author insight

MobileMe photo galleries are almost worth the annual subscription on their own. Yes, you can create online galleries free using other services, but that's not really the point. MobileMe galleries look fantastic, and they're perfectly integrated with iPhoto and its professional counterpart Aperture.

14.7 Find My iPhone

Find my iPhone could get you out of a hole if you lose your phone or you think it may have been stolen, and it also works with the iPad.

Find my iPhone is a tool which starts off looking rather odd but ends up looking as if it could be quite useful. Once you've registered your iPhone with your Mac, this tool is able to work out its location at any time, presumably by identifying the access point it's being used from. You can display a message asking whoever's using it for its return or, if that fails, you can wipe your personal data remotely.

14.8 iWeb

There's no iWeb panel on the MobileMe site, but it's still an important factor in deciding whether or not to take out a MobileMe subscription. Publishing directly to MobileMe may not be the only way to get your iWeb site online, especially now that iWeb 09 supports FTP uploading, but it's certainly the easiest.

Besides, there are certain features in iWeb, notably in blogs, which rely on special tools available only on the MobileMe web servers and not on others.

14.9 Synchronizing

MobileMe synchronization is taken care of by the MobileMe panel in System Preferences. You can choose what you want to synchronize and when (either automatically or manually). Apart from the data listed in this chapter, MobileMe can also synchronize Safari bookmarks, Dock items, Dashboard widgets and more. This is particularly useful if you use more than one Mac.

Author insight

MobileMe starts to make much more sense if you have an iPhone or an iPad or both. This is where the synchronization of data across all your devices really starts to pay dividends.

14.10 Is it worth it?

On the one hand, the annual subscription fee isn't a lot to pay for such a broad suite of Internet tools and the extent to which they can simplify your life and help you keep several different Apple devices up to date with the same information.

You may even decide that the iDisk, the web galleries and the iWeb publishing options are enough on their own to justify the fee. They don't do anything you can't achieve with free third-party services, but they look great and integrate so well with your Mac applications that they make life a lot easier.

But to get the full benefit of a MobileMe account, you really need to have taken on board the whole Mac ecosystem. You'll perhaps have two Macs – a desktop and a portable – and maybe an iPhone or an iPad too. If this is you, and you don't mind using your MobileMe account for your primary email address, MobileMe becomes very useful indeed.

14.11 iWork.com

This is a new online service introduced by Apple alongside iWork 09. It's designed to allow you to share iWork documents online with other users.

iWork.com is a new online collaboration tool available to MobileMe users. You can share iWork documents with co-workers, and they can view them and add comments using an ordinary web browser. Here's the chapter you're reading right now, created in pages and then displayed online using iWork.com.

What it does is display your iWork documents in a regular browser window – it doesn't matter whether the other person is using a Mac or a PC. The people you've invited to share your documents can leave comments which you can incorporate as you work on the document on your Mac.

Not only that, when you share via iWork, your Mac uploads not just a web version of the document, but the original iWork document and a converted version for Microsoft Office users. If you enable downloads, your co-workers can download the version most suitable for them and work on it or just store it on their own computers.

Will it catch on? It's very much like Google Docs, Google's online suite of office applications, but much more polished and designed to integrate seamlessly with the iWork apps on your Mac. When enough people get to see and understand what it can do, it could become an important collaborative tool for Mac users. These days, more and more of us are working with colleagues 'virtually' in different locations, and tools like these look set to become ever more important.

Author insight

iWork is a very interesting concept. It's easy to write it off as just another document sharing service until you try it out and see what it can do. What Apple has done, once again, is take a rather complicated need (online collaboration) and create an elegant and simple solution.

TEST

1 What's the difference between regular email accounts and 'web' mail?

2 Can MobileMe synchronize all your email accounts?

3 Why is MobileMe especially useful for iPhone or iPad users?

4 MobileMe can display your online photo galleries, but where do you actually create them?

5 MobileMe's iDisk currently offers 10Gb of online storage, but how do you access it?

6 What three things does Find My iPhone do to help when you lose your phone?

7 MobileMe has uses outside the six standard apps displayed when you log in, but can you name some?

8 Where can you find the MobileMe synchronization options?

9 iWork.com is a new online document sharing tool. But what happens if your co-workers don't have iWork, or don't even have a Mac?

10 Can co-workers download your iWork documents?

15

....

Dashboard widgets

In this chapter you will learn:
- *about the Dashboard*
- *what widgets are*
- *about the widgets which come with the Mac*
- *how to hide the widgets you don't want*
- *where to find many more widgets online*
- *how to download and install them*

15.1 What are Dashboard widgets?

That's a very good question! Widgets are like mini-applications which you can use for a whole range of jobs, from checking the definition of a word, to carrying out a quick calculation, to idling away a few spare minutes with a retro puzzle game. Widgets aren't opened like ordinary applications. They become visible only when you click the Dashboard icon on the Dock. All your widgets now become visible at once. Individually, they don't take up much space, and you can drag them around the screen into an arrangement which suits you.

You don't have to use the Dashboard icon to display your widgets, incidentally. If you're using an Apple mouse, open the Mouse panel of the System Preferences and check the actions assigned to the mouse buttons. The scroll button on a Mighty Mouse, for example, can be configured to activate the Dashboard when you press it.

It's easier to show what widgets do, than it is to try to explain them. We'll start with those that are supplied as standard. What we need to do, though, is split them into international widgets that are useful to UK users and US-only widgets which can safely be disabled as being of little use in the UK. The widgets that come with the Mac are of mixed usefulness, and you'll probably want to disable many of them. But there are many more widgets available online, and some of these really are remarkably clever.

First, though, let's deal with the standard widgets.

Address Book

This is just a small search box where you can type in the name of the person you want to look up in the Address Book. You may find it quicker than starting the Address Book application. Even as you're typing a name, the widget is listing matching contacts. When you click on a contact in the list, the widget displays the contact information.

Calculator

Need to work out the VAT on an invoice or the fuel consumption of your car? There's nothing fancy about this on-screen calculator, but it saves you having to rummage around in your desk drawers for a real one.

Dictionary

Need to know what a word means? Type it in and hit [**Return**] to get a definition, or choose Thesaurus from the pop-up menu to find other words with similar meanings.

Google

You can run a Google search using the search box in Safari, or you can do it here. When you press [**Return**], Safari launches to show the Google search results.

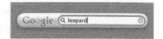

iCal

In its standard form, this just displays the current date and a mini-calendar. But if you click the date it expands to show upcoming events for the current day. Click on an event to launch iCal.

iTunes

This is a mini-console for iTunes, though given that iTunes has to be running for it to work, it's questionable how much use it is or how much time it saves.

Stickies

A yellow sticky pad you can use to jot down notes. You can change the font and the pad colour if you want to, but this is no word processor and its value, frankly, is limited.

Tile Game

Like the sliding tile games sold as novelties in toy stores – you have to assemble the picture properly by moving the squares around.

Translation

This one is very clever. It has two halves – in the top you type the word in English and in a few moments the translation appears in the bottom in the language you choose from the pop-up menu.

Unit Converter

Need to know how many pounds in a kilogram, or 65° F in Celsius? The Unit Converter has different sections for different types of conversion (area, weight and so on) and could prove quite useful.

Weather

It's easy enough to get a weather forecast from the television or online, but this saves you the trouble with a six-day forecast which uses icons to illustrate the expected weather graphically. Choose the nearest city to you by flipping the widget with its 'i' icon to show the settings on the back. Most locations are in the USA, but it does have British cities too.

World Clock

You can use this clock to display the time in any city in the world. Useful, maybe, if you regularly speak to colleagues overseas.

US-ONLY WIDGETS

Business

This is an American service similar to Yellow Pages in the UK. As such it's not really any use to Mac owners in the UK.

ESPN

Another American service, this time devoted to the latest US football, hockey, baseball and basketball results.

Flight Tracker

An airline flight-finding service that unfortunately doesn't work in the UK.

Movies

This one can find films playing in cinemas across the USA.

People

This is the American equivalent of the residential phone book in the UK.

Ski Report

Weather reports for the ski resort of Heavenly in California, anyone?

Stocks

You choose the stocks you want to follow by clicking the 'info' icon to spin round the widget and choose companies on the back.

Author insight

Widgets are simple and basic, that's their appeal. They're based on good ideas rather than complicated executions. If you like that approach, you'll love the style of the apps you can download for the iPhone and the iPad.

15.2 Configuring widgets

There are two aspects to configuring widgets. The first is how you adjust the widget's settings – we've already mentioned this once or twice. Nearly all widgets have a small 'i' icon, usually in the bottom right-hand corner. When you click this the widget is spun round to show the back, where these settings are made.

But you'll also want to decide which widgets are displayed and to get rid of those which you don't want.

1   If the Dashboard isn't visible already, click its icon on the Dock. You'll now see all your widgets appear on the screen and your other applications will fade into the background.

2   With the Dashboard active, if you look in the bottom left-hand corner of the screen you'll see a large round button with a '+' symbol in the middle. You need to click this...

3   This opens up a horizontal widget bar at the bottom of the screen. This lists all the widgets currently installed on the Mac and not just the ones which are currently visible.

4   To display any of these widgets, click their icon in this bar. If you don't see the widget you want, use the arrow buttons at either end of the tray to scroll left or right to see more.

5 You'll note that in this mode each widget visible on the screen has a round '+' button in the top left-hand corner. To get rid of a widget, click this button to close it. It's not deleted from the system – it's still there on the tray – but it's not displayed on the screen any more.

6 To remove widgets from the widget bar, click the **Manage Widgets** button near the tray's top left-hand corner. All your widgets are now displayed in a list, and you can click the checkbox alongside any widget to deselect it and remove it from the widget bar.

7 Widgets can be deleted completely by clicking the red button to their right in this list. You can only do this with widgets you've down-loaded and installed yourself, though, and we look at these in the next section.

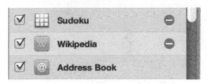

Author insight

Widgets are a lot of fun, but you might feel there's something about them that doesn't quite gel. Perhaps the biggest problem is that they're slightly inaccessible – you need to activate the Dashboard, which temporarily deactivates what you're working on. Plus the fact that they're all displayed at once, which means the screen is full of clutter once you've chosen half a dozen favourites.

15.3 Where to get more

The widgets supplied as standard with the Mac are a bit of a mixed bunch, but they are just the tip of the iceberg. Many, many more can be downloaded from the Apple website. They come from a whole range of sources, from big companies to self-taught programmers working from a bedroom. And while some are highly-specialized, others can be brilliantly useful, entertaining and inventive.

To find and install more widgets:

1 Open the **Manage Widgets** dialog (see step 6 above), and click the **More Widgets** button. This takes you to Apple's widget website. Or, start Safari and type the link into the Address Bar – www.apple.com/downloads/dashboard.

2 Ignore the **All Downloads** list on the left. Instead, look for the row of links under the **Dashboard Widgets** heading and click **Categories**.

3 Let's say you want to check out some games. Click the **Games** category to see a list of games widgets which runs, incidentally, over several pages.

4 To view more about a widget, click its title. You'll see a short description and find out whether it is freeware or a shareware/demo release. Most are freeware – free to download and use. Some are shareware, which means they run in trial mode for a while but later you'll have to pay to carry on using them. Some widgets are demos, which means some of the features are disabled until you pay for the full product – there is often a lot of crossover between 'shareware' and 'demo' software.

5 When you find a widget you want, click the **Download** button. Safari's **Downloads** window will show the download in progress, though widget files are very small and the download will be finished almost as soon as it's started.

6 When it's completed you'll be asked if you want to install the widget and open it in Dashboard – click the **Install** button.

7 You now get to try out the widget before pressing the **Delete** or **Keep** button. If you keep it, it's added to your list of widgets.

Searching for widgets is so absorbing, and the widgets themselves so simple and inventive, that you can spend hour after hour doing nothing but trying them out – you have been warned!

15.4 Favourite widgets

Here are four of the author's favourite widgets. These are just a few of the many thousands out there, so these are only examples of what's possible, not a definitive list of the only ones worth having.

CodeBreaker

A version of the classic puzzle where one player lines up a row of pegs of different colours and the other has to guess what they are with a series of guesses that gradually narrow down the options. Here, the Mac creates the code and you make the guesses.

Depth of field Calculator (DOFC)

A widget for photographers who want to calculate the depth of field (near to far sharpness) in a photograph. Highly technical, but to those who need it, a tool which sidesteps a lot of tedious calculations or complicated tables.

Sudoku

The classic number puzzle which has sold a million paperbacks can now be played on your Mac Desktop. It's perhaps not quite the same as scratching away with a pencil in your favourite armchair, but it's great for addicts.

Wikipedia

The Wikipedia website is a great place to look up information on any subject, but this lets you do it without having to start Safari and navigate to the Wikipedia site. Articles are displayed in the widget window, which can be expanded if necessary.

TEST

1 *How do you display your widgets?*

2 *Is there a widget shortcut?*

3 *Most widgets can be configured with a variety of settings... but how?*

4 *How do you display all the widgets currently installed (and not just those which are visible)?*

5 *How do you hide widgets you don't want without uninstalling them?*

6 *How do you remove widgets completely?*

7 *What are 'freeware', 'shareware' and 'demos'?*

8 *Where can you get more widgets?*

16

....

Games and utilities

In this chapter you will learn:
- *about games for the Mac*
- *where you can get them from*
- *how to download game demos*
- *how to find and play games online*
- *how to preview electronic documents*
- *how to compress files for storage or emailing*
- *what you can do with Stickies*
- *things you can do with Photo Booth*

16.1 Game types and top sellers

You don't normally buy a Mac just to play games. Serious gamers would invest either in a PC with an expensive and powerful graphics card or a dedicated games console like the PlayStation 3 or Xbox 360.

Having said that, there are more games available on the Mac than you might think, and some up-to-date best-selling titles too. You won't see them much in the shops because dealers concentrate heavily on the most common formats and don't usually devote shelf space to minority computers. But Mac games are widely available online if you shop at www.amazon.co.uk, for example. Do make sure you check the system requirements first, to make sure that your Mac has the hardware needed to run the game – and in particular that it has the right graphics card.

You may have already tried out the Chess game on the Mac, and the selection of Big Band board games. These, though, are just the start. So what kind of games can you buy for your Mac?

COMBAT GAMES

These usually consist of first-person action (you see the game through the combatant's eyes) and a series of missions which you have to complete, or a more strategic approach to battlefields where you make command decisions instead. Some games combine elements of both.

These games can be both involving and addictive. Examples include Medal of Honor (excellent first-person combat combined with suspense and tactics), Call of Duty (equally highly regarded) and Quake (18 only).

Mac games are hard to find in the shops but you can get them from big online retailers like Amazon, including the highly-regarded Call of Duty series.

SIMULATING LIFE

Here, you're attempting to run a game world using a set of complex rules which mirror those in real life. You can either have missions where you must reach certain goals, or you set your own goals and try to achieve them.

Sim City was one of the earliest Sim games but it has spawned many sequels. It's very complex and involving, though perhaps

The Sims series is great fun and lets you mimic real life in the comfort and safety of your own home. Sims 3 Ambitions is the latest expansion pack (it adds features to the original game).

a little dry for those looking for a little light entertainment. If that is what you want, The Sims is a better bet. Here, you control cartoon characters in a cartoon world, trying to improve their careers and even their relationships. It's like practice for real life (almost)!

DRIVING GAMES

Modern computer hardware has made a big difference to driving games, and examples in this genre include the excellent Colin McRae Rally and Need for Speed, plus TOCA Race Driver 3, though, admittedly, there aren't as many Mac driving games as there are strategy/wargames (though kids might like to try out Disney Pixar Cars).

There aren't too many driving games on the Mac because these are mostly found on games consoles, but TOCA Race Driver 3 is worth seeking out.

STRATEGY AND ROLE-PLAYING

Some game genres, such as driving games, action shooters and sports simulations are better-suited to games consoles, but cerebral strategy and role-playing games still work well on desktop computers like the Mac.

Current top-seller is StarCraft II: Wings of Liberty. You can play the part of one of three different races, tackling a range of very different 'story missions'. The online gameplay option adds another dimension as you get to play against human opponents – computer opponents are tough but sometimes predictable, whereas human opponents keep evolving and changing their tactics.

Strategy games like StarCraft II provide an utterly involving and challenging game-world where you need brains as well as brawn.

16.2 Where to get Mac games

www.amazon.co.uk and other online software retailers are a good place to get Mac games, but you can also find out what's available by visiting www.apple.com/uk/games. Here you can find out about the latest games releases and discover whether games which are famous on the PC are also available in Mac versions.

Many games are made available as downloadable demos, and while the file sizes can be very large, with a broadband account they will still download quite quickly. To find out what's available, go to www.apple.com/uk/downloads/macosx. You should see a list of categories on the left where you can select Games. This heading now expands to show a list of sub-genres, so just click on the one you're interested in (Action & Adventure, for example). Now you can look through page after page of games, clicking on anything that looks interesting to get a short description and a screenshot.

These games are a mixture of full commercial releases being distributed in a demo form, shareware games from smaller companies who distribute their software online rather than as boxed retail software, and some freeware games written just for the fun of it by amateur programmers.

And don't forget the Mac's ever-growing supply of widgets (see Chapter 15). Widgets are mostly free, and there's a huge range of games to try. Obviously these aren't going to be as elaborate as a full-scale commercial game, but they can still be very absorbing and entertaining nonetheless.

Looking for Mac games? Go to www.amazon.co.uk and type 'Mac games' into the search box.

Author insight

There are lots of games you can play on a Mac, but to be honest the best ones are simple no-brainers designed to offer a few minutes' distraction. If you're really into games, you're going to be better off with a console.

16.3 Games widgets

Games don't have to be complicated to be fun. If you're a less demanding games player just looking for a bit of a distraction between jobs, or a game that doesn't tax your grey cells too much, then don't forget the Mac's widgets.

There are lots of fun games you can download as widgets, many of them free. See the previous chapter for more on finding and downloading widgets. The Apple site's widgets section has a whole category devoted to games.

Mac widgets won't any prizes for technical sophistication, but there are lots of free games which can prove maddeningly addictive.

16.4 The Apps Store

If you have an iPhone or an iPad, you'll probably already know about the Apps Store, where you can browse and download thousands of different applications. Many are free, many more cost just a couple of pounds/dollars.

Some of the games available have startlingly good graphics, and if you're looking for a short diversion rather than a long-term hobby, they can be terrific value for money.

It's just a shame that you can't play iPhone and iPad games on a regular Mac!

16.5 Mac utilities

The Mac comes with a number of utilities, which you can think of as software designed to do general odd jobs. We won't cover all of them here because many are highly technical and may never be used.

Preview
This is an application which the Mac uses to display image files when you double-click them in the Finder. You can zoom in to check for sharpness or even double-click several images and display them as a slideshow.

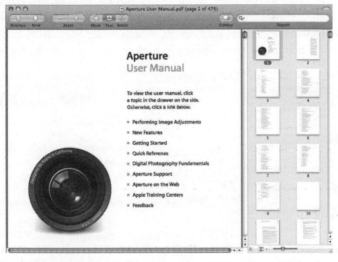

The Preview utility is Apple's alternative to Adobe Reader, and you use it to read electronic documents and manuals in the PDF format.

Preview also opens PDF files, doing the same job as the Adobe Acrobat Reader. Many manufacturers supply manuals as PDF files on CDs that come with the product, rather than providing printed manuals (electronic manuals are a lot cheaper). Here, Preview displays the document pages in the main window and thumbnail versions of the pages in a panel on the right to help you go quickly to the page you want. There's also a search box for finding specific text within the document.

Author insight

Preview is Apple's alternative for Adobe's Acrobat Reader.
Both programs display electronic documents in the PDF
format but, it has to be said, Acrobat makes a bit of a meal
of it, with complicated features (unused by most of us) and
frequent online updates.

Compressed .zip files

This isn't a utility as such, but a feature built into the Mac OS.
On Windows computers you commonly compress a whole series
of files into a single zip file to make it easier to email them to
someone else. On the Mac, to do the same thing: select all the
files you want to zip, hold down [Ctrl] and click on any of the
highlighted files – then choose **Compress xxx items** from the menu.
This produces a compressed zip file which other Mac users can
open to retrieve the files. These zip files can be opened on PCs, too.

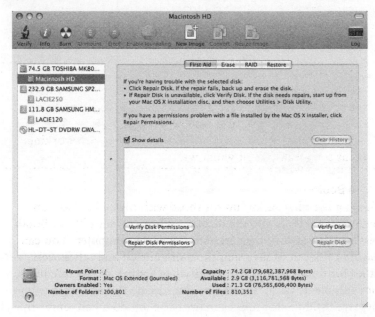

Disk Utility helps you repair disk faults, format disks and 'partition them' (for when you use Boot Camp, for example).

Disk Utility

This can be found in the Utilities subfolder in the Applications folder. You can use it to check and repair disks which appear to be giving problems, and also to erase (format) disks to wipe them clean. Disk Utility can also partition disks so that they appear and behave like different disk drives in the Finder (the total capacity will be the same as the physical disk itself). Partitioning is used when setting up a Mac to run Windows with Boot Camp.

Stickies

The Stickies widget can also be found in the Applications folder. It displays sticky notes on-screen which work in just the same way as the real thing, only you don't get sticky marks on the screen and they don't fall off in hot weather. You can change the size of a sticky by dragging on its bottom right-hand corner, and you can create as many new stickies as you like. The contents of stickies are saved when you quit the program and reappear the next time you use it. You can also export the text of a sticky note (or copy and paste it) for use in another program.

Author insight

We mention Stickies as one of the Mac's Dashboard widgets, but it's also a fully-fledged application. This version is a lot more useful because you can create many sticky notes at once, and you can float them over whatever you're working on as semi-transparent windows.

Photo Booth

This is a harmless bit of fun for those with Macs that have an iSight camera built into the display. When you start Photo Booth, what you see is your own face staring at the computer. You can use Photo Booth to save snapshots of yourself and other users, either for fun or to add mugshots when setting up user accounts, for example. It's also possible to record video clips, and save both these and still photos to iPhoto or send them to other people by email. There are some special distortion effects you can apply too, and it's amazing how much puerile fun you and your friends can have with such a simple tool.

Photo Booth uses the camera built into the display of many Mac models. Use it to grabs stills or videos and have some fun with the special effects.

Author insight

Maths students should take a look at Grapher in the Applications folder. It's a utility for generating 2D or 3D graphs from mathematical equations which you can use for visualization or export as images.

17

Multiple users

In this chapter you will learn:
- *what a user account is*
- *how to password-protect a Mac*
- *the advantages of individual user accounts*
- *how users' files are kept private and separate*
- *how one user can swap files with another*
- *how to enable fast switching*

17.1 Your user account

You may be used to thinking of a computer as something that simply starts up and works, but today's operating systems are designed with multiple users in mind, and with protecting the privacy of each of these users. You may be the only person in the house or office who uses your Mac, but in most homes a single computer may be used by several different people. What you don't want is for all these different people to meddle with the settings and poke around with each other's files.

That's why the Mac OS, like Windows, is specifically set up to cater for multiple users. Each user has his or her own username and password, and when they've logged on it's as if the Mac is theirs. They see only their own home folder and not anyone else's and, by the same token, the files in their home folder cannot be seen by others. It's also possible for different users to choose their own desktop pattern and other Mac preferences without affecting those of other users.

Author insight

If you're used to storing files where you like on your computer's hard disk, then user accounts and the need to use a 'home' folder can seem like a tiresome restriction. You soon adapt, though, and it's worth it for the extra security and the ability to share one computer between two or more people.

You may not need to set up multiple accounts. You may indeed be the only person using your Mac. Nevertheless, it's important to understand that this system exists because it means that certain Mac features and jargon will then make sense.

For a start, you have a user account on your Mac, even if you are the only user. You can see this if you open the System Preferences and choose Accounts in the System section. The account will be under your name and labelled Admin. This means that you have Administrator privileges for changing settings on the Mac. You can do anything you like, in other words.

It's not essential to enter a password for this account, but it is a good idea, because if your Mac is ever lost or stolen it will provide a certain basic level of security that won't stop a skilled hacker but would probably defeat a casual thief. But this will not work if the Mac is set for Automatic Login. This is the simple but lazy option! When the Mac is set up for Automatic Login, it'll start up without demanding your password.

With Automatic Login disabled, the Mac will list the available user accounts when it starts up, and you'll have to enter the password for the account you want to use. To do this, click on the Login Options button at the bottom of the list of user accounts.

It's a nuisance to have to type this in each time you start your Mac, but it's a worthwhile precaution, especially with a portable MacBook or MacBook Pro.

This option can be found in the Accounts panel – click the account name on the left to select it, then click the Login Options button below (you may need to click the padlock icon in the bottom left-hand corner of the window to unlock the settings). Now just make sure the Automatic Login pop-up shows Disabled.

To set or change a password:

1. Go back to the Accounts panel and click the **Change Password** button.
2. Type in the old password (if any).
3. Type in the new password then type it a second time to make sure the spelling is consistent.
4. If you forget your password you won't be able to start your Mac, but there is a failsafe mechanism built in – a password hint. Type a word or phrase that will jog your memory. If you do forget your password, you'll be able to look up this password hint from the Login window.

Now while you were in the Accounts window back there, you'll probably have spotted that you can set up additional accounts using the '+' button in the bottom left-hand corner. This is ideal if other family members need to use the computer, but you don't particularly want them to have access to your files (or each other's). And this is what we'll look at next.

If you want to password-protect your Mac, go to Accounts in System Preferences and disable the Automatic login within the Login Options.

Author insight

If you're the administrator, it's a good idea to make a note of the passwords you set up for other users on that computer. Otherwise, if you forget (or if they don't want to tell you), it can be difficult to fix things later if they go wrong.

17.2 Adding a user

Let's imagine your daughter needs to use the Mac for her college coursework.

1 Make sure the padlock, bottom left, is unlocked so that you can make changes.

2 Click the **New Account** ('+') button bottom left.

3 This opens the **New Account** panel with a series of boxes that must be filled in. First, though, note the pop-up menu at the top. This lists the account types available. The most powerful is an Administrator account, but since you want to be the only one able to control the Mac's settings, you should choose Standard instead.

4 First, type in the new user's name. The **Short Name** box below will be filled in automatically.

5 Now type in a **Password** and confirm it in the box below and, just to be on the safe side, a password hint in the box at the bottom. Click on **Create Account** to finish.

There are two significant aspects to what you've just done. The first is that when the Mac is started up, it will display both users on the screen, so that either of you can log on (it will require the correct password for each user account).

The second thing to note is that the new user has their own home folder with their own Pictures folder, Music folder, Documents folder and more. Each user can use the Mail application, for example, but they'll only ever see their own mail, and no one else's.

Other people's home folders are visible in the Finder in the Users folder, but only the current user's home folder has the home icon, and access to the others is barred.

Author insight

Different user accounts can be useful even if it's only you that's using the Mac. For example, you might want different home and work accounts to separate what you do outside office hours from your 9–5 job. It looks better if you're presenting work to colleagues or clients, too, if you don't have lots of personal stuff visible alongside it.

Privacy is taken very seriously in the Mac OS. Even those with Administrator accounts can't access the contents of users' home folders without their password. Of course, you could always insist you choose the password when you create the account, but the more democratic thing to do is turn your back for a moment while the new user types it in.

Different users can't see each other's files, but they can exchange files using the other person's Drop Box.

There is a way for different users to exchange files, though, and that's via Drop Boxes. There is actually one folder in another user's home folder which you can access. Open their Public folder. You'll see a Drop Box folder – you can drag items into this. Similarly, other users can leave items for you in your own Drop Box.

Author insight

Each user has their own music collection, their own iPhoto library, their own documents folder and their own desktop image and screensaver. It's a neat system which allows everyone to set the computer up according to their own preferences without affecting anyone else.

17.3 Switching between users

It's very useful for different people to be able to use the same computer while still keeping their files private, but it would be a nuisance if you had to shut down and restart the computer each time. Fortunately, you don't have to. You can switch users while the machine is running, and there are two ways of doing this:

1 Open the Apple menu and choose **Log Out**. This closes any applications currently running and returns you to the Login window and its list of users.
2 The quicker option is to go back to the **System Preferences** and the **Accounts** panel, unlock the padlock in the bottom left and click **Login Settings**. Now check the **Enable fast user switching** box.

3 You'll see the current user's name at the right-hand end of the menu bar at the top of the screen. When you click this, you'll see a list of all the users. To switch users, click another name.

The Mac will prompt you for that user's password, then switch to 'their Mac'. With fast switching, each user's documents and applications remain open, so you can switch back to the previous user and they can pick up exactly where they left off.

Indeed, when you set up multiple user accounts, it really is as if each person has their own Mac. The whole process of setting up accounts and passwords may sound a bit of a nuisance, but it's simpler and quicker than it sounds and really is the perfect solution for a 'family' computer.

Author insight

You can create accounts with a 'Simple Finder' for young children who might find the real thing a bit intimidating and choose which applications are available. These are part of the Parental Control options.

TEST

1 What's the 'home' folder?

2 Why set up different user accounts? Why not just store files where you like on the hard disk?

3 Why bother with a password if you're the only user?

4 How do you stop your Mac from starting up automatically?

5 What's the difference between 'Admin' and 'Standard' user accounts?

6 How can different users share files if they can't see each others' data?

7 You can choose the user account when you start the Mac up, but do you have to shut it down again to choose a different one?

8 What's the advantage of 'fast user switching'?

System Preferences

In this chapter you will learn:

- *how to configure and personalize your Mac's display*
- *about screen savers and customizing the Dock*
- *about hardware preferences*
- *how to apply parental controls to user accounts*
- *how to activate the Mac's speech options*
- *how to make a Mac easier to use for those with visual or hearing impairments*

18.1 Personal Preferences

The Mac's System Preferences are mentioned many times throughout this book, and they're used to control many aspects of the Mac, like the Control Panel on a Windows PC. Many of these will never need changing, but it's still useful to know what they're for. They're split into four sections, and the first is devoted largely to the Mac's appearance and behaviour. You can configure these to customize your Mac.

Appearance

Many people will use their Macs for months or years without knowing (or caring, perhaps) that it's possible to change the look of parts of the interface. Here, though, you can change the colours used for highlighting, the position of scrollbars and the way text is rendered on the screen.

Desktop & Screen Saver

Here you can choose from a wide range of abstract desktop patterns or colours. (You can also set a desktop image directly from iPhoto.) If you don't like the standard screen saver (it can start to pall after a while), change it for another, like Word of the Day, which puts random definitions on the screen.

Dock

Normally, the Dock runs along the bottom of the screen, but you can align it vertically to the left- or right-hand sides. If you check the Magnification box, icons enlarge as you move the mouse pointer over them, which can be fun (for a while). And if you check the Automatically hide and show the Dock box, it slides out of the way when you're not using it and only reappears when you move the mouse pointer to the bottom of the screen.

Expose & Spaces

Expose is a Finder tool for showing all your open windows at once.
It does this by shrinking them and displaying them side-by-side on
the screen. This makes it easier to locate and switch to a window
when there are lots open at once. Normally, you press [F9] to make
this happen, but you can change this so that just moving the mouse
pointer to the corners of the screen will do it. Also, this is where
you configure the Spaces feature.

Language & Text

The language for your Mac will be set up when you first configure
it, but it's also possible to change the language settings here later
on. This panel also sets date and time formats, the type of calendar
in use (e.g. Gregorian), units of measurement and the first day of
the week (e.g. Sunday or Monday).

Security

There are three tabs in the Security panel. In the General tab you can set the Mac to request a password when it's woken from sleep or screensaver mode. In the FileVault tab you can opt to encrypt your home folder so that the data cannot be viewed without a password – the encryption is stronger than regular user passwords. There are other options, but they are outside the scope of a basic guide.

Spotlight

This is the Finder's search tool, and it will look in the listed locations for the words you type. You can deselect the areas you don't want to search, to save time or because they are irrelevant.

18.2 Hardware Preferences

CDs & DVDs

In this panel you decide what you want the Mac to do when you insert a blank CD or DVD. By default, for example, the Mac opens blank CDs in the Finder but asks you what you want to do with blank DVDs. If you want these to open in the Finder too, or in another application, you choose that option from the pop-up menu alongside.

Displays

LCD displays only have one native resolution, and this will be selected automatically by the Mac. However, there may be instances where you need to select a lower resolution for screenshots to illustrate an article, for example. In the Color tab it's possible to manually calibrate the brightness and colour of your display against on-screen samples. This can help you get more accurate colours from some displays.

Energy Saver

Macs have different Energy Saver settings according to the model type and the situation. These are probably most useful with MacBooks and MacBook Pros, where you need to preserve battery power carefully when away from a mains supply. Using this panel you can set the Mac to go to sleep, set the display to sleep or power down the hard drive if it's not been used for a few minutes (the delay can be adjusted over a wide range).

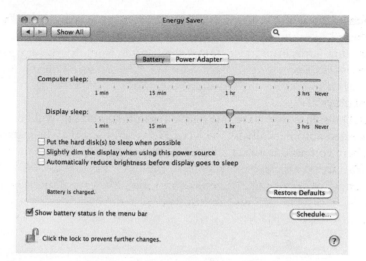

Keyboard

You may never need to change any of these settings, but at least you'll know where they are and what they do. You can use the Keyboard panel to adjust the repeat rate of the keys and check or disable keyboard shortcuts.

Mouse

You can use this panel to control the operation of your mouse. The Apple Mighty Mouse, for example (seen here) can be set up to work as a one- or two-button mouse. The top scroll button is clickable too, as are the two side buttons.

Trackpad

If you struggle with the Trackpad on a MacBook, use the Trackpad panel to experiment with the tracking speed and other settings.

Print & Fax

This panel shows any printers connected to the Mac and, if there's more than one, you can choose the default. This is the printer that appears first when you attempt to print from any application. If you click the Options & Supplies button, it may also be possible to check how much ink is remaining.

Sound

In the Sound panel's Sound Effects tab you can try out different alert sounds for your Mac, and in the Output tab it's possible to change the left–right balance of the speakers and the output volume – though you can also check the Show volume in menu bar option so that the volume control is available all the time (besides, Mac keyboards have volume control keys anyway). The Input tab allows you to adjust the input volume of the built-in microphone and that of the Mac's Line in input, where used.

18.3 Internet & Wireless

These Preferences control the Mac's network and Internet connections and how files and folders are shared with others.

MobileMe

If you don't have a MobileMe account, this panel is irrelevant. If you do, you can use it to check your account status, choose which items are synced with MobileMe and when, and monitor how much of your available iDisk space remains unused.

Network

The settings available here are technical and quite advanced, and with any luck you won't need to change any of them. The Mac connects to other networks automatically, but where you encounter problems and need to contact a technical support department, you may be asked to check and modify some of these settings.

Bluetooth

This is used to check the configuration of any Bluetooth devices connected to the Mac. The most obvious example of this is the wireless version of Apple's Mighty Mouse, but many mobile phones can also connect and swap files and other data.

Sharing

This controls how some of the more advanced sharing tools are configured, e.g. whether other (authorized) users are allowed to view and control your computer remotely. Many users will want minimal sharing options, if any, and these can be selected from the list on the left. File Sharing, Printer Sharing and Bluetooth Sharing is probably as far as most people will want to go.

18.4 System Preferences

Here you can set up user accounts, set the Mac's internal date and time and adjust the operation of Leopard's Time Machine backup tool

Accounts

We covered user accounts in some depth in Chapter 17, so we won't repeat it here. This is the panel where user accounts are set up and administered.

Date & Time

If you need to check or reset the Mac's date and time, this is where you do it. You can also configure the clock display on the menu bar, swapping from analogue to digital, for example.

Parental Controls

If your Mac is used by many different family members, you may at one time or another be concerned about the websites they might be visiting or how long they're spending on the computer. With this panel, you can modify each user account to carefully control this usage, and it's surprisingly easy to do.

Software Update

These days, applications don't wait for you to check whether updates are available. They check for you at regular intervals and prompt you to install any new updates. This applies to the Mac operating system too. Here you can configure how often update checks are made, and you can also examine a history of previously-installed updates (although for Apple software only).

Speech

It's possible to control your Mac and some of its applications using voice commands! It's not enabled as standard, though, because while this kind of technology is certainly a novelty, it lacks the speed and precision of conventional mouse/keyboard input. Your Mac can also read out text in computer voices which make a good stab at sounding human, and there are several to choose from in the Text to Speech tab. Want to try it? Choose a key combination unlikely to be used by any other software (e.g. **[Ctrl]**-**[Alt]**-**[Command]**-**[S]**). Select any text on the screen, use this key combination and wait for the Mac to start talking.

Startup Disk

You'll only need this panel if you're using Boot Camp to turn your Mac into a PC, or if you need to start up from a DVD or network drive to carry out diagnostics and fault-finding.

Time Machine

Time Machine is Leopard's and Snow Leopard's backup tool, and here you can switch it on or off and choose the external disk drive used for the backups.

Universal Access

The Mac has a number of options for helping those with eyesight or hearing difficulties. It can display text larger on the screen, read out options when the mouse pointer is moved over them and flash the screen instead of playing an alert sound.

TEST

1   Having the Dock at the bottom of the screen on a widescreen display can make the display even narrower. What can you do about it?

2   How do you change the Mac's currency units, or the day the week starts on?

3   You can set the Mac to require your account password when it emerges from sleep or screensaver mode, but how?

4   How do you make your Mac start its DVD player automatically when you insert a DVD?

5   How do you calibrate your monitor's display manually?

6   Your MacBook shuts down too quickly when it's not being used. What can you do about it?

7   Can you control the amount of time your family members spend on the computer?

8   If you suffer from visual or hearing difficulties, the Mac has tools to help, but where are they?

Answers

Chapter 1

1 The processor family makes the most difference, and you can only really compare speeds within that family.
2 You can get by perfectly well with 2Gb. More RAM will speed things up, though, and is needed for some professional applications.
3 There are 1000 (strictly speaking, 1024 gigabytes, but that's just splitting hairs).
4 The Mac Mini.
5 The iMac.
6 Eight – two quad-core Xeon processors working in parallel.
7 MacBook Pros offer a choice of display sizes, they come with 4Gb RAM as standard and they can be upgraded to 8Gb.
8 It's more expensive and a little less powerful, but it's under 2cm thick when closed and weighs only 1.36kg.
9 No, it has to use software written especially for it, though there are already tens of thousands of programs.
10 Yes. Leopard and Snow Leopard have a feature called Boot Camp which let you start up your Mac as a PC, though you will have to buy and install your own copy of Windows.

Chapter 2

1 It might look like they've only got one, but Mac mice respond to pressure on both sides. You can choose whether the mouse acts like a traditional single-button Mac mouse, or as a twin left/right button mouse using the Mouse panel in the System Preferences.

2 Just hold down [Ctrl] as you click the mouse button. This temporarily turns it into a 'right-click'.

3 The menu bar is separate and fixed to the top of the screen, regardless of the position of the program window(s). It's a different way of doing things, but you very quickly get used to it.

4 You just drag it off the Dock and it disappears. It's still available in the Applications folder – the icons on the Dock are simply shortcuts.

5 They're little mini-applications for odd-jobs or mindless entertainment. They can be a lot of fun, but you may find you never use them.

6 List view. It's worth trying out the Column view, though, because you may eventually come to prefer it.

7 The Home folder is a secure section of the hard disk set aside for a particular user. Home folders allow different people to use the same computer without ever being able to see or access each others' files.

8 Use the Mac's Spotlight feature. The Mac keeps an index of all the files and folders on your hard disk, updating it automatically as you work. Think of it as a search engine for your Mac!

9 Use the Mac's Force Quit feature – [Alt]–[Command]–[Esc]. This displays a list of the programs currently running and will usually highlight the one that's frozen. You can 'force quit' this program without affecting the others.

10 Just close the lid. When you open it up again, the Mac will return to the state it was in when it went to sleep, complete with all open applications and windows.

Chapter 3

1 No, because the software 'drivers' may be different. The vast majority of plug-in peripherals are both Mac and PC compatible, though, and some devices like USB drives and external hard disks are generic.

2 USB is a universal standard used by computer and peripheral makers worldwide. FireWire is a similar but incompatible connector used principally by Macs and some plug-in devices. USB is by far the most common method for connecting devices.

3 You can connect using an Ethernet cable and the Ethernet socket on the back of the Mac, or you can connect wirelessly using the Mac's built-in wireless connectivity.

4 Lasers cost more to buy but they are good for high-volume low-cost printing, and produce printouts which don't need to dry. Inkjets cost less to buy and are better for low-volume, high-quality printing, especially photos.

5 Yes, you can, using a FireWire cable and the Mac's iMovie software, which is compatible with the majority of digital camcorders.

6 From the USB cable you use to connect it to the Mac. USB ports also provide power, though if you're using a USB hub it will need its own power supply.

7 Time Machine. It uses an external hard disk to maintain constant backups in the background as you work.

8 USB flash drives. They're cheap and they're everywhere. Even a 1Gb drive holds more than a CD and you can re-use it as many times as you like.

9 Traditionally, PC keyboards connect with a special PS2 connector which the Mac doesn't have, but many modern keyboards connect via USB and these will work fine. You can use USB mice designed for PCs too.

10 It's called the Magic Mouse, it connects via Bluetooth instead of a cable, and the single-piece top surface acts as both a one- or two-button mouse and supports scrolling too, by touch alone.

Chapter 4

1 Stacks are displayed at the right-hand end of the Dock and their contents can be displayed as a Fan, Grid or List.

2 It's a way of displaying and skimming through the files in a folder as large-scale previews of the file contents.

3 On the Finder sidebar.

4 They display specific files and types according to search criteria you set up when you create the Smart Folder.

5 Select the file in the Finder and hit the spacebar. The Quick Look feature displays its contents as a large-scale preview.

6 It's called 'Spaces', and it sets up two or more alternative displays. It's like having two computers running at once on the same screen and being able to toggle between them.

7 It's called Time Machine, and all you need is an external disk drive with around twice the capacity of your Mac's hard drive. Once Time Machine is set up, it runs on its own, automatically, without any further intervention.

8 Yes it can, thanks to a feature called Boot Camp which lets a Mac start up as PC. You will need to buy and install a copy of Windows, though.

9 It's called Safari, but you don't have to use it. Firefox and Google Chrome are equally effective.

10 As long as you haven't emptied the Trash, you can open it up and drag out your file. And in Snow Leopard, you can 'restore' it to its original location.

Chapter 5

1 A modem will only connect one computer to the Internet, but a router will provide an access point for two or more.

2 Not always. Most require a username or password to prevent unauthorized use, while others may carry a charge, depending on where you are (hotels and cafes, for example).

3 No. Firefox is available in both Mac and PC versions, as is Google Chrome. Both are very good alternatives and work in a very similar way.

4 It's called Bing, and you can find it at www.bing.com.

5 A username and a password. No transaction can be completed without both of these, and you can choose what they are when you set up your account with the retailer.

6 They let you open other web pages in addition to the one you're on, but without creating a new browser window. You can look at these different web pages by clicking on their tabs.

7 For this you need a 'web' mail account, and you can get these free from Yahoo, Google and others. You view your mail using a web browser, and all your messages are stored online rather than being downloaded to the computer.

8 The Address Book. This is a list of names, numbers and addresses used by a number of Mac programs, not just Mail. You can add people to your Address Book very easily when they send you an email, just as you might add contact information to your phone when you get a text.

9 If you mark it as junk in the Mail program, it will get better at recognizing and filing away junk automatically.

10 An email which pretends to be from a company you deal with and tries to trick you into sending (or 'confirming') your password or username for a bank account, for example.

Chapter 6

1 Word processor documents are the usual sort. Pages are added automatically as you write and the layout options are limited. Page layout documents are different. Here, you choose the page designs you want and type your text into boxes. Here, Pages is taking the place of a traditional desktop publishing program.

2 Open the Media panel and click on the Photos tab. This displays the contents of your iPhoto library, complete with all the folders and albums you've set up.

3 It's dummy text or pictures placed on a template to show you what the layout will look like. You type directly over the placeholder text and drag your own photos on to the placeholder pictures to create your documents.

4 A slide. These can be thought of as individual 'screens' of information, and you build up your presentation using a series of these slides.

5　Transitions control how one slide blends into the next (with a 'fade' or a 'wipe' effect, for example), while animations control how individual objects on the slide appear or move.

6　They're called Masters, and they're chosen using the Masters button on the toolbar, which displays a drop-down list of designs.

7　In Numbers, data is stored in 'tables'. You can have more than one on a single sheet and you can make them exactly the size you need.

8　Click on the empty cell directly below and insert the SUM function.

9　'Formula'.

10　You can open Microsoft Office files directly, but to create a file that Microsoft Office can open, you have to use the Export command to convert them into a form that the Office programs can read.

Chapter 7

1　In the Project Gallery. This can be set up to display automatically whenever you start Word, Excel or PowerPoint.

2　Outlining. It's a special mode where headings can be arranged in a hierarchy of ideas and information, which makes the rest of the writing process much easier.

3　Inline graphics are embedded in the text, and if the text moves due to changes elsewhere, the graphics move too. Floating graphics stay in the same location and the text flows around them according to the text wrap settings you choose.

4　Publishing Layout mode.

5　Lists. These store data in rows which can be sorted, filtered and subtotalled.

6　This is a pop-up menu which Excel can generate automatically from column headings when you create a list. It's an extremely fast and straightforward way of isolating and summarizing data.

7 You can also display your presentation as an outline, where each heading corresponds to a slide title. This makes it much easier to organize your ideas, and it's very similar to the outlining feature in Word.

8 They're notes you can add to each slide for your own reference when making a presentation, but which are not visible to the audience.

9 Slide Layouts control the content of each slide, such as the number and position of text boxes, picture elements and so on. Slide Themes control the appearance, including fonts, backgrounds and colour schemes.

10 A Mac version of Outlook, which is the personal information manager in Microsoft Office on the PC.

Chapter 8

1 Email (as attachments), file transfer websites (e.g. www. yousendit.com), CDs or DVDs, USB flash drives, networks.

2 They're slow to prepare, their capacities are not particularly high by today's standards, and they're not very 'green' since they can (usually) be used only once.

3 They're inexpensive, they can be re-used indefinitely and they come in higher capacities than either CDs or DVDs.

4 From the USB cable used to connect it to the computer. There's no need for a separate power cable, and that's what makes them so convenient.

5 Yes, but it has to be formatted for a PC (FAT32 format) first.

6 Access is restricted to folders you nominate for sharing, and you can use passwords to restrict access further.

7 Save it in a common format that both programs can read. For example, JPEG files for photos, the Word format for text documents, Excel format for spreadsheets and so on.

8 It's the 'zip' format, and both Macs and PCs can save and open zip files.

9 In order to retain compatibility with PCs when swapping files.

10 If you know the file type, tell them to type the extension in manually after the filename (e.g. .tif, .doc, .txt).

Chapter 9

1 It can do either. By default, it imports them into its own internal library (useful if you import pictures from memory cards), but you can also set it up to refer to them in their current location on your computer.

2 It scans your photos for human faces so that you can identify the individuals concerned. It then learns to recognize individuals automatically in the future.

3 It's a system for embedding location data (a set of co-ordinates) in a photo so that programs like iPhoto can place it on a map.

4 With an album, you manually choose which photos you want to add to it. Smart albums automatically display photos which match certain criteria, such as keywords and ratings.

5 It's a word or a short phrase you might use often to describe a photo, such as 'holiday' or 'family' or 'landscape'. Keywords make it easier to find specific pictures later.

6 You could sort your pictures in order of their rating, so that they best ones appear first, and you can use ratings as one of the criteria for smart albums.

7 Go into Full Screen mode, then move the mouse pointer to the bottom of the screen to display the toolbar. Click the Adjust button to display the manual editing controls.

8 It means that you can make changes to your photos, but they're not permanent. You can go back at any time to undo them or adjust the settings.

9 Create a Slideshow album using the New Album command on the File menu. You can now choose from a range of pre-designed slideshow Themes.

10 If you have a MobileMe account you can upload albums directly as an online gallery. You can also export photos to the iWeb application. Finally, you can Export photos as simple web albums from within iPhoto.

Chapter 10

1 The iPhone and the iPad.
2 You don't. iTunes does it automatically, using each audio CD's unique identity to look up its artist, title and song names in an online database.
3 They come from the iTunes store, and they're either applied automatically when you buy music from the iTunes store or you can download them yourself or albums you've imported.
4 With a regular playlist, you add the songs you want manually. With a smart playlist, you specify the artist, the rating, the album name or a whole range of other criteria, and iTunes finds matching songs automatically.
5 The Equalizer works like the graphic equalizers on hi-fi systems – you can adjust the volume of different frequencies to change the quality of the sound. The Visualizer is harder to describe – it's like an animated screensaver pattern set to music.
6 iTunes displays the total playing time of the currently selected playlist at the bottom of the window.
7 It's all right if you have an iPod Classic or a large-capacity iPod Touch, but there may not be enough room on an iPod Touch or a Nano for all your music.
8 Currently, 99p.
9 On the iTunes store, in the Podcasts section. They consist of audio and video episodes, and many podcasts are free.
10 Radio stations which 'broadcast' over the Internet rather than radio waves, so that you can listen to radio stations anywhere in the world without having to be within transmitter range.

Chapter 11

1 iDVD is a special application which assembles movies into ready-to-play DVDs complete with menu screens.

2 You can import movie files already transferred to the Mac's hard disk, or you can import movies direct from camcorders/cameras.

3 'Standard' HD is 1280 × 720 pixels, while 'full' HD is 1920 × 1080 pixels.

4 In the Event Library.

5 Create a Project and then add the clips you want to include from the Event Library.

6 Move the mouse pointer left and right over the clip to 'skim' through at whatever speed you like. Then stop moving the mouse and hit the spacebar to preview it from that point.

7 You choose a transition and then drag it into the gap between the two clips in the Project window.

8 They're screens containing text, graphics or both which you can use to introduce your movie and separate different sections.

9 Any Mac with a built-in microphone. If you're using a Mac without a microphone, make sure you buy the right type from a Mac supplier (ordinary types aren't suitable).

10 That's easy. iMovie can export videos for YouTube and, if you have a MobileMe account, you can export movies to a MobileMe gallery too.

Chapter 12

1 Click the thumb tack button in the bottom right corner of the iCal window.

2 To move an appointment, drag it from its centre. To change its duration, drag its top or bottom edges.

3 With an on-screen reminder or an email message.

4 To separate your work and home calendars, for example, with the ability to view them individually.

5 Go to the day you want, then drag the To Do on to the calendar. You can then move it and adjust the start/finish times as necessary.

6 Apple Mail. You will often want to create To Do items while checking your mail.

7 It also stores phone numbers, addresses and even notes about colleagues, contacts and friends.

8 They're a way of creating mini-collections of people in specific categories, for example 'friends', 'workmates' and 'customers'.

9 You can send out bulk emails to many people at once by addressing them to the group rather than to individuals.

10 With Smart Groups you don't add people manually, but specify search criteria for people to be added automatically, such as contacts who live in London.

Chapter 13

1 What You See Is What You Get. In iWeb you can simply put things where you want them to appear, and the complicated web design code needed is generated automatically behind the scenes.

2 You can open a Finder window on top of iWeb and drag a photo on to the page, or open the Media panel, which will display the contents of your iPhoto library.

3 These are lines which appear as you move objects around to help you snap them into alignment with what's already on the page. It makes your pages look much neater and more 'designed'.

4 The Navigation bar. It's generated automatically at the top of all your web pages, and each time you add a new one it's added to the bar. Your site's visitors can use this to go to different pages.

5 Websites are a structured set of pages linked together. Blogs are a sequence of pages added one by one, like an online journal.

6 Blogger (www.blogger.com) and WordPress (www.wordpress.com).

7 It stands for File Transfer Protocol, and it's a standard way of downloading files or, if you're publishing a website, uploading them.

8 iWeb 09 now has an option for uploading your sites to a web server using built-in FTP transfer, where previously you would have had to export your files to your hard disk and use a separate FTP program.

9 A company which will put your website online in exchange for a monthly fee or subscription. MobileMe is, amongst other things, a web hosting service.

10 They're bits of code you can insert into boxes on your web pages. They can do different things, like displaying Google Maps, a MobileMe photo gallery or a YouTube video.

Chapter 14

1 With a regular email account, mail is downloaded to your computer using an email program. With web mail, your messages are stored online and you can view them and reply using any computer.

2 No, and this is an important limitation that Apple doesn't explain clearly. It can synchronize mail for your MobileMe account, but not any other accounts with other providers. It only works well when you use MobileMe for your primary email address.

3 It synchronizes mail, contact and calendar information across all your devices. If you add a phone number on your iPhone, for example, it's synchronized back to your Mac's Address Book.

4 iPhoto. You can upload them directly to MobileMe without leaving iPhoto, and any changes you make in iPhoto are synchronized to the MobileMe gallery.

5 There are two ways. First, click on the iDisk icon in the Finder sidebar. The iDisk looks and works like a regular disk drive. Second, use MobileMe online. The iDisk interface looks slightly different but works in the same way.

6 It can locate any registered phone on a map, it can display a message to anyone who uses it and it can remotely wipe personal data if necessary.

7 We've already mentioned iDisk, but you can also publish iWeb sites directly to MobileMe, and the new iWork.com service lets you share your iWork documents with others.

8 In the MobileMe System Preferences panel.

9 It doesn't matter, because iWork converts your documents into a form which can be viewed on any browser. Visitors can't edit documents directly, but they can leave comments which you can integrate with the document on your Mac.

10 Yes, if you enable this option when you share them online. iWork creates both iWork and Microsoft Office versions.

Chapter 15

1 Click the Dashboard icon on the Dock.

2 Check the Mouse panel of the System Preferences. You can configure it to activate the Dashboard by pressing the scroll button on the top or by squeezing the side buttons inwards (Mighty Mouse).

3 Look for a small 'i' icon which appears when you move the mouse pointer over the bottom corner. This flips the widget round, and you'll find the settings on the 'back'.

4 Click the '+' button which is visible in the bottom left-hand corner of the screen when the Dashboard is active. This displays the 'widget bar'.

5 When you display the widget bar (see above), each widget shows a '+' icon in the top left corner. Click on this to hide the widget (it will remain visible on the widget bar if you decide to add it again later).

6 Click the Manage Widgets button at the left end of the widgets bar. This displays the Manage Widgets window, where you can delete widgets you don't want by clicking the red button to the right of the name. You can only delete widgets you've downloaded yourself, though.

7 Freeware is software you can download and install for nothing. Shareware and demos are programs which can be downloaded for nothing, but which are missing key features or can only be used for a certain amount of time, for example 30 days. They are designed to let you try the software out before you buy it.

8 From the Apple website, either directly at www.apple.com/downloads/dashboard or by clicking the More Widgets button in the Manage Widgets window.

Chapter 17

1 It's a private folder on the Mac which contains all the files associated with your own personal account on that computer.

2 With user accounts, several people can use the same computer, but keep their own files separate and private from the rest, and even customize the display wallpaper and other options according to their tastes.

3 It stops other people starting up your Mac. A determined hacker could get round the password, but it will stop casual thieves and snoops from prying into your data.

4 Select Login Options in the Accounts panel and choose 'Off' from the pop-up Automatic log-in menu.

5 The Admin account is the most powerful and gives you full control over the computer (and setting up other user accounts). A Standard account allows others to use the computer freely, but without the Administrator's level of access.

6 Each user has a Public folder and within this is a Drop Box. Other users can see this and drop files into this Drop Box. They can't see its contents, but the owner can, and can copy these 'dropped' files into their own folders.

7 No, you can switch users while the Mac is running. Open the Apple menu and choose the Log Out option. This closes all running applications and returns you to the Login screen you see when the Mac starts up.

8 When this is enabled, you can swap users without having to quit what you're doing. The original user's programs stay running exactly as they were left, and work can be resumed later when the user is switched back again.

Chapter 18

1 You can open the Dock panel and either set it to hide automatically (it only appears when you move the mouse pointer down to the bottom of the screen), or fix it to the side of the screen instead.

2 The Language & Text panel.

3 You'll find this in the Security panel, in the General tab.

4 If it doesn't do this already, open the CDs & DVDs panel and choose this option in the pop-up menu.

5 Use the Color tab in the Displays panel. (Be warned, though, that it's difficult to improve on the standard Mac monitor's colour rendition.)

6 Open the Energy Saving panel and adjust the power-saving options and time delays.

7 Use the Parental Controls panel, which lets you choose settings for each person's user account.

8 In the Universal Access panel.

Glossary

Airport Apple's name for the Mac's wireless networking hardware. It hooks up seamlessly to standard PC wireless networks and routers.

Bit The basic building block of digital data. A bit is either 1 or 0, but by stringing bits together it's possible to store much more complex data.

Blog A web journal where new entries are posted in chronological order and old entries are stored in a searchable archive.

Bluetooth A short-range wireless communications system that's not fast enough for proper networks or Internet connection, but fine for things like wireless keyboards and mice.

Broadband Modern digital communications system using conventional phone lines but with digital data transfer that's much faster than old-fashioned modems.

Burn CDs and DVDs store data optically not magnetically, so you can't save data to them in the same way you'd save it to a floppy disk. The data has to be burned (literally) into the surface.

Byte 8 bits strung together. One bit has only two possible values, one byte has 256.

Clock speed The number of processing cycles a processor carries out each second. It's a good indicator of a processor's performance when compared with another of the same type.

Context menu or shortcut menu One devoted to specific objects on the screen and activated by clicking the right mouse button or holding down [**Ctrl**] when you click the left button.

Dialog A window which prompts you for more information or to make a choice. For example, when you save a file, the Save dialog will ask you what you want to call it and where you want to save it.

Dial-up connection Pre-broadband Internet connection where the computer's modem would have to dial up the Internet host computer over the telephone line.

Driver A software file which allows hardware devices to communicate with the computer. Many devices come with software, including drivers, which you must install before they can be used.

Ethernet Networking system for computers in the same room or building. May be wireless or wired (using cables).

File sharing Making files on one computer accessible to other computers on a network.

Firewire A means of connecting computers and peripherals. Similar to USB, but the two are incompatible. Now rarely used, though still a standard way of transferring footage from digital camcorders.

Folder A container for files and other folders on a computer and a way of keeping things organized. Rather like the folders in a filing cabinet, but here you can have folders within folders within folders and so on.

Freeware Software which is given away, usually by programmers trying to make a name for themselves or as a promotional tool for software companies.

FTP (File Transfer Protocol) A standard system for managing files and folders on a host computer over the Internet.

Gigahertz A measurement of clock speed in a computer. Today, 2 gigahertz (GHz) is average, 3Ghz is good, though outright speed also depends on the processor family/type.

Hardware The physical bits of the computer – circuit boards, screens, keyboards, printers.

iLink Another name for Firewire connections on camcorders.

Ken Burns effect Adds the appearance of motion to still images by slow panning and zooming and subtle transitions.

Memory stick See stick drive.

Menu bar A list of menu titles running horizontally across the top of the screen. You click on a menu title to display the menu.

Minimize The yellow button in the top left-hand corner of a window shrinks it into a little icon on the Dock. The window hasn't gone away – you can click the icon to show it again.

Modem Device which converts computer data into a form which can be transmitted across telephone lines, and back again into data. May be built into the computer or plugged in as an external device.

Navigate Move from one location (folder) on your hard disk to another, either within a program in an application, or within the Finder. Also used for menus, as in 'navigate through the menus'.

Operating system If the computer's hardware is its body, this is its brain. You, and the programs you use, interact with the operating system, which then controls the hardware. From time to time, manufacturers will upgrade this operating system with new tools or fixes for things that didn't work properly.

Palette A collection of tools or an informational display which can be moved around the screen into the most convenient position or closed completely when it's not needed.

Peripheral Any external device you plug into a computer.

Phishing Emails which appear to be from known companies, like your bank, and ask you to confirm or supply confidential user information or passwords.

Podcast Audio or video programme which is made available for downloading from the Internet rather than broadcast. So called because it was originally conceived by Apple as broadcasts for the iPod.

POP email accounts POP is the standard protocol for handling email messages which you download to your computer using an email program.

RAM (Random Access Memory) The computer's temporary thinking space. Most computers are shipped with the bare minimum, and adding more can speed up many processes.

Router A device which handles the data traffic between computers on a network, 'routing' it to the right machines.

Scrollbar These appear at the right and the base of a window when it's too small to show the full contents of the file. You can use the scrollbars to see the other parts of the file.

Search engine A website whose sole purpose is to help you find information on other websites. You type in a word or phrase and the search engine finds all the sites that mention it.

Shareware Software that's distributed freely, but which you're expected to pay for if you want to carry on using it once you've tried it out.

Sidebar Vertical panel on the left of the screen in many Mac programs, which is designed to offer quick access to common tools or locations.

Sleep mode Reduced-power mode where the computer powers down the display and drive, but doesn't actually shut down. When you 'wake' it, you can start work just where you left off.

Spam Unsolicited email which is trying to sell you things, tempt you with get-rich-quick schemes or, occasionally, trying to trick you into giving personal details ('phishing').

Stick drive Solid state memory devices which plug directly into a USB port and can be used for transferring files to other computers. Usually no larger than a small key fob.

Surfing Browsing the Web, generally with no particular destination in mind.

Terabyte We're used to measuring hard disk capacity in gigabytes (millions of megabytes), but some drives are now over 1000 gigabytes – and 1000Gb is a terabyte.

Toolbar Horizontal strip of buttons and drop-down menus, usually displayed below the menu bar and designed for a specific and related set of operations. You might have a toolbar for adjusting text formatting in a word processor, for example.

USB interface A standard means of connecting computers to external devices. A USB cable connects the USB socket on the device to the USB port on the computer.

Virtual memory If the computer doesn't have enough random access memory to complete a task, it temporarily transfers some data to the hard disk to make room. This is virtual memory – it's not quite the same as the real thing, being dramatically slower, for a start.

....

Widget Small software tool designed to do a simple job quickly.

....

Wireless hotspot Any area within wireless range of a router or other access point with an Internet connection.

....

Index